Y0-AWJ-842

DATE DUE

970.01 Gaffron, Norma   c.1
GAF   El Dorado, land of   21322
        gold

HILBERT JR. HIGH LIBRARY
26440 PURITAN
REDFORD, MICHIGAN 48239

GREAT MYSTERIES

El Dorado, Land of Gold

OPPOSING VIEWPOINTS®

Look for these and other exciting *Great Mysteries: Opposing Viewpoints* books:

Alternative Healing *by Gail Stewart*
Amelia Earhart *by Jane Leder*
Anastasia, Czarina or Fake? *by Leslie McGuire*
Animal Communication *by Jacci Cole*
Artificial Intelligence *by Erik Belgum*
The Assassination of President Kennedy
  by Jeffrey Waggoner
Atlantis *by Wendy Stein*
The Beginning of Language *by Clarice Swisher*
The Bermuda Triangle *by Norma Gaffron*
Bigfoot *by Norma Gaffron*
Custer's Last Stand *by Deborah Bachrach*
Dinosaurs *by Peter & Connie Roop*
The Discovery of America *by Renardo Barden*
El Dorado, Land of Gold *by Norma Gaffron*
ESP *by Michael Arvey*
Evolution *by Marilyn Bailey*
Jack the Ripper *by Katie Colby-Newton*
Life After Death *by Tom Schouweiler*
Living in Space *by Neal Bernards*
The Loch Ness Monster *by Robert San Souci*
Miracles *by Michael Arvey*
Noah's Ark *by Patricia Kite*
Pearl Harbor *by Deborah Bachrach*
Poltergeists *by Peter & Connie Roop*
President Truman and the Atomic Bomb
  by Michael O'Neal
Pyramids *by Barbara Mitchell*
Reincarnation *by Michael Arvey*
Relativity *by Clarice Swisher*
The Shroud of Turin *by Daniel C. Scavone*
The Solar System *by Peter & Connie Roop*
Stonehenge *by Peter & Connie Roop*
The Trojan War *by Gail Stewart*
UFOs *by Michael Arvey*
Unicorns *by Norma Gaffron*
Vampires *by Daniel C. Scavone*
Witches *by Bryna Stevens*

GREAT MYSTERIES

El Dorado, Land of Gold

OPPOSING VIEWPOINTS®

NORMA GAFFRON

Greenhaven Press, Inc.   P.O. Box 289009, San Diego, California 92198-0009

No part of this book may be reproduced or used in any form or by any means, electronic, mechanical, or otherwise, including but not limited to photocopy, recording, or any information storage and retrieval system, without prior written permission from the publisher.

Library of Congress Cataloging-in-Publication Data

Gaffron, Norma, 1931-
    El Dorado, land of gold : opposing viewpoints / by Norma Gaffron.
      p. cm. — (Great mysteries)
    Includes bibliographical references and index.
    Summary: Presents opposing views of experts on the myth of the lost city of gold sought by Spanish explorers in fifteenth century and by some modern treasure hunters.
    ISBN 0-89908-086-3
    1. El Dorado—Juvenile literature. 2. America—Discovery and exploration—Spanish—Juvenile literature. [1. El Dorado. 2. America—Discovery and exploration—Spanish.] I. Title. II. Series: Great mysteries (Saint Paul, Minn.)
E123.G24   1990
970.01'6—dc20   90-3838
                                                 CIP
                                                  AC

© Copyright 1990 by Greenhaven Press, Inc.

*Dedicated to Terry O'Neill,
understanding editor, and warm friend.*

*"Where can it be — this land of
 El Dorado?"*

*"Over the mountains of the moon,
 Down the Valley of the Shadow."*

—*Edgar Allen Poe*

Contents

	Introduction	9
One	A Golden Man	10
Two	Golden Dreams	16
Three	A Legend Takes Shape	40
Four	The Dream Becomes an Obsession	50
Five	A Mixture of Fantasy and Reality?	86
Six	The Lure of El Dorado	100
	Bibliography	107
	Index	109
	Picture Credits	111
	About the Author	112

Introduction

This book is written for the curious—those who want to explore the mysteries that are everywhere. To be human is to be constantly surrounded by wonderment. How do birds fly? Are ghosts real? Can animals and people communicate? Was King Arthur a real person or a myth? Why did Amelia Earhart disappear? Did history really happen the way we think it did? Where did the world come from? Where is it going?

Great Mysteries: Opposing Viewpoints books are intended to offer the reader an opportunity to explore some of the many mysteries that both trouble and intrigue us. For the span of each book, we want the reader to feel that he or she is a scientist investigating the extinction of the dinosaurs, an archaelogist searching for clues to the origin of the great Egyptian pyramids, a psychic detective testing the existence of ESP.

One thing all mysteries have in common is that there is no ready answer. Often there are *many* answers but none on which even the majority of authorities agrees. *Great Mysteries: Opposing Viewpoints* books introduce the intriguing views of the experts, allowing the reader to participate in their explorations, their theories, and their disagreements as they try to explain the mysteries of our world.

But most readers won't want to stop here. These *Great Mysteries: Opposing Viewpoints* aim to stimulate the reader's curiosity. Although truth is often impossible to discover, the search is fascinating. It is up to the reader to examine the evidence, to decide whether the answer is there—or to explore further.

"Penetrating so many secrets, we cease to believe in the unknowable. But there it sits nevertheless, calmly licking its chops."

H.L. Mencken, American essayist

One

A Golden Man

In ancient times, according to the Chibcha people of South America, a beautiful goddess named Bachu rose from the icy waters of Lake Guatavita. At her side was a child. Together the goddess and her son wandered the mountains and valleys of the Chibcha land, teaching the people how to grow corn, how to build shelters, and where to mine fabulous treasures of emeralds and gold.

After a time, their work done, Bachu and her son returned to the lake. The people wanted to show their gratitude to the goddess, so they created a spectacular religious ceremony in her honor. Once a year, before dawn on the first day of spring, the Chibcha people assembled before the dwelling of their *cacique* (chief). When he appeared, they smeared him from head to foot with a sticky layer of balsam gum. Then they puffed powdered gold through tubes of cane over the gum until the chief glittered in the rising sun.

They covered their *El Dorado*, or Golden Man, with a red robe. On his face they placed a mask of gold and emeralds. Strong warriors lifted their cacique onto a throne. At the edge of the lake, they placed the throne upon a raft. As the sun rose higher in the sky, the warriors rowed the raft out into the center of the lake. There the cacique let his robe fall onto the raft. Then, lifting his arms to the heavens, he stood, like a living

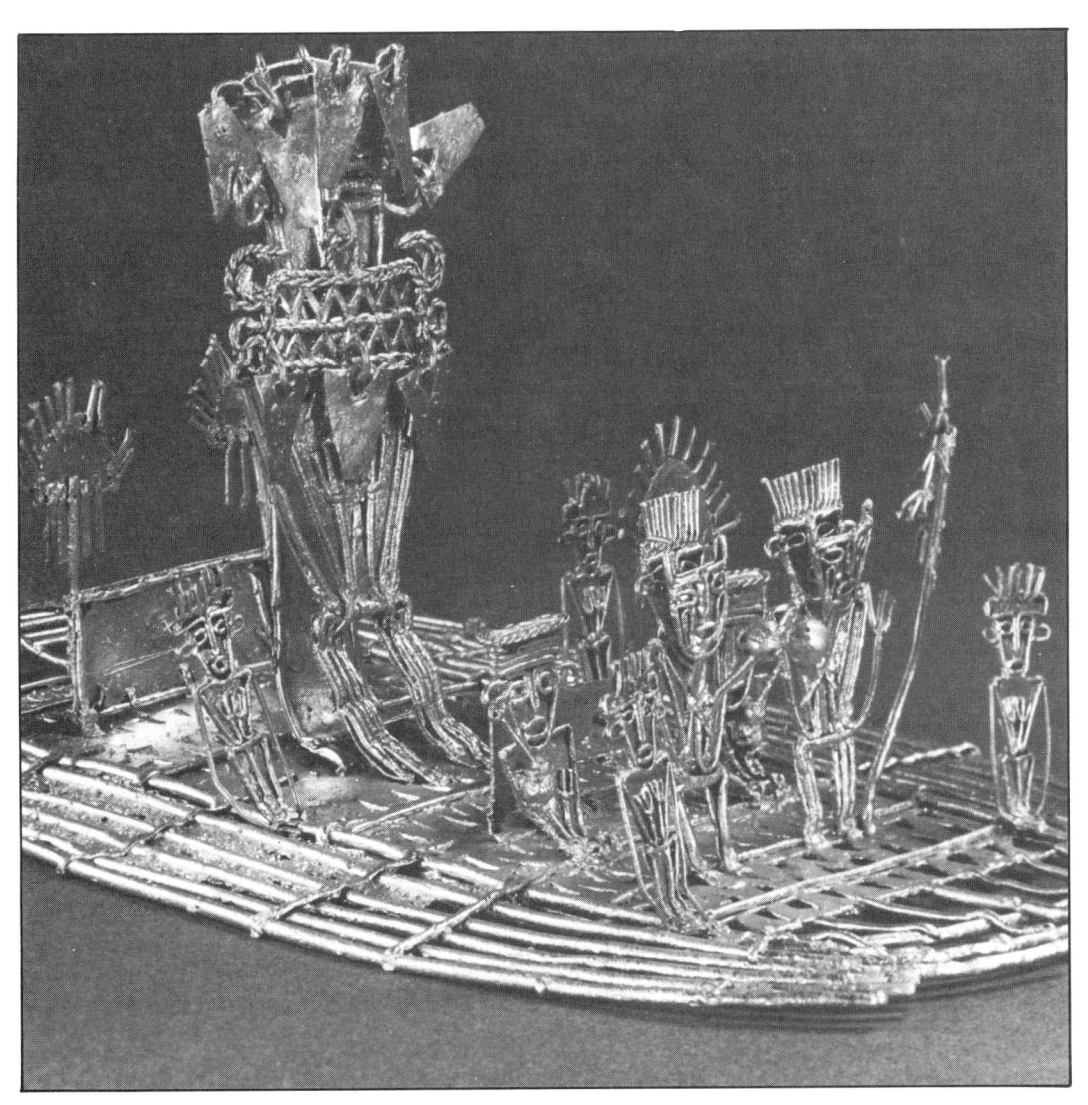

This golden raft is a *tunjo*, a ceremonial offering. This tunjo depicts the ritual of the Golden Man. It shows the gilded king being rowed to the center of a lake. There the king will dive into the lake where the gold dust will wash off into the water as a sacrifice to the gods.

statue of gold! He took off his golden mask and dropped it into the deep waters of the lake. He dropped figures of gold and emeralds into the lake, too. Finally, the cacique dove into the cold water and the gold dust washed from his body as a last offering to the goddess of the lake.

When he swam back to the raft, the cacique was again wrapped in his red robe. He was rowed to shore, and feasting began.

Amid the sounds of flutes and shell trumpets the people danced, sang, and drank chicha (a corn-based liquor) until the sun left the lake of Guatavita in darkness.

A Legend and a Symbol

Did a golden cacique ever really exist? Did rituals such as this ever happen? Author Timothy Severin, writing about El Dorado in his book *The Golden Antilles*, indicates that they did. "About the year 1480 the splendid ceremony at Lake Guatavita [in northern Colombia] was snuffed out when a hostile tribe invaded the area and defeated the practitioners of this strange rite." Severin

This drawing was made by Theodor de Bry in about 1599. De Bry never travelled to America, but his drawings, based on the tales of those who had been there, helped establish European ideas about America. In this illustration, he shows Muiscas (a South American tribe) blowing gold dust on their cacique, or chief.

writes that the spectacle was far too brilliant to be forgotten, however. He believes it became entwined in the folklore of other South American natives, and as they retold the story they added elements of fantasy.

The elaborate details often recounted might easily have been added by those who had never seen the fabulous ceremony at the lake. Some versions said the king ruled over a golden city whose palaces were sheathed with plates of gold. His soldiers wore golden armor. The nobility were decorated like their cacique, in crusts of powdered gold, whenever the court held its week-long banquets. In one version of the story, the golden objects thrown into the lake went not to thank a kind goddess, but to appease a terrible monster. In other versions the ceremony took place only when there was a new ruler. It is possible that some differences resulted because similar ceremonies may have taken place in other lakes.

Author Victor W. von Hagen in *The Golden Man* calls these stories of a Golden Man "factual myths" because they are based in fact but have grown into myth. Others refer to them as legends, stories that come down from the past but cannot be proved.

Legend, myth, or reality, stories of the Golden Man and his golden kingdom expanded over the years, and eventually found their way to Europe in the sixteenth century where life was harsh and starvation and disease were commonplace. Naturally, tales of fabulous wealth were appealing. Explorers had been coming to the New World ever since Christopher Columbus arrived in the Antilles in 1492, but tales of the golden treasures of this new world inspired even more exploration.

Explorers were enchanted by the blue water, the gentle breezes, and the soft scenery of the countries surrounding the Caribbean Sea. The

"El Dorado does not have and never had any foundation."

Juan de Castellanos, sixteenth-century chronicler

"The Golden Man was a fact—a factual myth."

Victor W. von Hagen, *The Golden Man*

GULF OF MEXICO
Sargasso Sea
WEST INDIES
Cuba
Hispaniola
Puerto Rico
Jamaica
Greater Antilles
Mexico
CARIBBEAN SEA
Trinidad
Gulf of Darien
VENEZUELA
PACIFIC OCEAN
COLUMBIA
Guyana Highlands
Lake Guatavita
EQUATOR
ECUADOR
Amazon
BRAZIL
PERU
Matto Grosso
BOLIVIA
PARAGUAY
CHILIE
ARGENTINA
URUGUAY

virgin soil was rich and deep, so crops grew readily. This was indeed a "golden land," blessed by the sun.

As if that were not enough, the natives wore ornaments of gold, and they played with green stones which the Europeans knew to be valuable emeralds! The story of El Dorado only added to the mystery and charm of a place already considered to be something of a paradise. Hundreds of adventurers came looking for the king so rich he wore gold dust and threw treasures into a lake. They came too, to find the golden city. Did it really exist? Or was it a myth? If it was real, where could it be found?

The Land of Gold

For centuries people have been seeking El Dorado. Even today people search for El Dorado in the large, unexplored areas in the heart of South America. Originally "the golden one," the name in time came to mean any place where unimaginable riches awaited those who could find them. In short, El Dorado (often spelled as one word), has come to mean paradise. It may be a symbol for something that can never be found.

But no one has found El Dorado, the Gilded Man, or El Dorado the kingdom of riches and dreams. Hundreds of people have lost their lives looking for it. Perhaps more will.

What inspires them? What keeps them looking?

Will they ever find El Dorado?

Opposite: The search for gold has taken travelers all over the world. In the Age of Exploration, many seekers focused their efforts in mid-America—Mexico, Central America, and northern South America.

Two

Golden Dreams

"The powerful mystique of gold originally had much to do with its colour," writes author Jennifer Westwood in *The Atlas of Mysterious Places*. "The Egyptians linked [gold] to the sun and to the life-essence.... In West Africa, [in ancient times]... a pinch of gold dust tucked into a dead man's loincloth was his passport through the spirit world." Gold was the ultimate treasure, guarded in fairy tales by dragons. It has always been rare—the total ever mined is reckoned at less than a million tons, according to Westwood. No wonder Christopher Columbus wrote:

> Gold is the most exquisite of all things.... Whoever possesses gold can acquire all that he desires in this world. Truly, for gold he can gain entrance for his soul into paradise.

Holding such a philosophy, it is not surprising that Columbus became the first link between El Dorado and the countries of Europe.

Christopher Columbus and the New World

Christopher Columbus sailed west from Spain in 1492, just twelve years after the last ceremony at Lake Guatavita is supposed to have taken place. Columbus had not heard of the Golden Man, but he had heard tales of fabulous riches in Cathay (China), Cipangu (Japan), and India. These oriental countries were known as the Indies. Very few of their treasures of gold, jewels,

Theodor de Bry depicted South American Indians mining gold, but the European explorers could not find these elusive mines. Perhaps they were mythical.

The fleet of Christopher Columbus. Columbus's search for a new way to the Orient sparked the European search for gold in the New World.

and spices reached Europe, since merchants traveling to and from the Far East had to make their way over thousands of miles of treacherous mountains and through endless deserts, facing hostile tribes on the way. Columbus vowed he would find a waterway across the Ocean Sea (the Atlantic Ocean) to cut down the time and eliminate some of the dangers of getting riches from the Orient.

For financial help, he went to the king and queen of Spain. He promised that he would claim in their names any land he found. In addition, he would determine whether the people there could be converted to Christianity. But Columbus was dedicated first of all to adventure. He said his greatest wish was "to learn the secrets of the world." It was soon obvious that the secrets he most wanted to learn were the origins of the gold and precious stones thought to be found on the islands of the Indies.

Marco Polo, an Italian traveler and author, had described China (though he had never been there) as "richer than any [country] yet discovered.... It possesses gold and silver and precious stones in large quantities." He mentioned the large island of Japan also, calling it an unknown place with "temples and palaces covered in gold." These writings not only inspired Columbus but convinced him that the discovery of a better route was worth any effort!

Arrival in Paradise

Columbus and his crew did not have an easy time crossing the Ocean Sea, but they finally dropped anchor in the Bahamas. Columbus must have been ecstatic! Surely these small islands were the gateway to Japan! He recorded his findings and his feelings in letters to King Ferdinand and Queen Isabella. On Saturday, October 13, 1492, he wrote:

> At daybreak great multitudes of men came to the shore, all young and of fine shapes, and very handsome.... [They came to the ships in small canoes] loaded with balls of cotton, parrots, javelins, and other things too numerous to mention. These they exchanged for whatever we chose to give them. I was very attentive to them, [and] strove to learn if they had any gold. Seeing some of them with little bits of metal hanging at their noses, I gathered from them by signs that by going southward or steering round the island in that direction, there would be found a king who possessed great cups of gold.... I tried to get them to go there but found they were unacquainted with the route.

Since Columbus believed he was near Japan, one of the countries called the Indies, he dubbed these natives "Indians." He thought that it might be possible to find some gold on their small island, but, he wrote, "So as not to lose time, I am determined to see if I can find the island of Cipangu."

So off he went, with no clear idea of how far away this king with the cups of gold could be found, or if what the Indians said was true.

"Columbus spoke of a river near Santo Domingo full of gold nuggets 'of such quality it was a marvel.' "

John Hemming, *The Search for El Dorado*

"El Dorado...was a dream fed by the excitement of discovering a new world."

Thomas Dickey, *The Kings of El Dorado*

P: B: Bouttats fec. Aqua fort

Columbus sailed from island to island in the Caribbean Sea, naming them and planting crosses on them, claiming them for Spain. The first island he landed on he named San Salvador. The island we know as Cuba he called Juana, in honor of the daughter of Ferdinand and Isabella. Though it was big, he decided this was not Cipangu because he found no gold palaces there. On Hispaniola (Haiti) he at last found gold in quantity. The natives gave him and his crew small chunks of it, handing them out as if they were trinkets of little value.

The explorers' excitement mounted, for a messenger arrived on Hispaniola bearing gifts from a nearby king. One of the gifts was a mask with ears, nose, and tongue of hammered gold. His king, said the messenger, lived near the source of this glistening metal. The king invited Columbus to visit him on his island.

A Happy Accident

On the evening of December 24, 1492, Columbus sailed north for what he felt must be Cipangu. He should have waited until morning. In no more than an hour, his ship, the *Santa Maria*, struck a coral reef. The friendly king of Hispaniola came to Columbus's rescue. He tried to comfort Columbus by hanging a plate of gold around the admiral's neck. Seeing the happy response, he comforted the visitor further by trading more gold for Spanish clothing (for which he had little need, as the people of Hispaniola usually went naked). The trading went on until Columbus had enough gold to impress the queen. On January 4, 1493, he set sail for Spain aboard the ship the *Niña*. He left thirty-nine of his men on the island with instructions to collect gold from the mines they would surely find before his return.

"Columbus was now certain that he had

Opposite: Columbus and his crew land on Hispaniola and receive rich gifts from the natives.

Columbus convinced Queen Isabella and King Ferdinand that investment in voyages to the New World would be lucrative for Spain.

found the Indies," writes historian Samuel Eliot Morison, in *The Great Explorers*. But, although Columbus made three more voyages to America, explored the coasts of Central and South America, and eventually reached the mainland of North America, he did not find a sea route to India and Japan. Nor did his men find gold mines on Hispaniola or on the other islands.

Yet there was no doubt that rich deposits of precious metal existed somewhere in this vast new land. Perhaps the explorers were not looking in the right places. Indeed, it was the explorers to the south who found the first substantial quantities of gold.

On the Mainland of South America

In 1501, just nine years after Columbus first landed in the New World, Rodrigo de Bastidás and Juan de la Cosa visited the northern coast of what is now South America. Bastidás was a Spanish merchant from Seville, and de la Cosa was a former navigator with Columbus. The two men discovered and named the harbor of Cartagena.

Bastidás and de la Cosa traded with the chiefs

of this area, which was called the Sinú region. They sent a good quantity of golden objects back to Spain by ships. King Ferdinand was so impressed that in 1508 he authorized the first attempts at settlement of the mainland. The people who settled there were to concentrate on the search for gold mines.

"The ultimate dream of every conquistador [Spanish conqueror] was to discover a gold or silver mine that would yield a steady flow of treasure," according to John Hemming in *The Search for Eldorado*. But these adventurers had other objectives also. Some were looking for fertile land on which to make a new life—to find that symbolic El Dorado, or paradise. Others were still looking for a waterway that would enable them to get spices from the Orient. "All the early expeditions started with one of these objectives," writes Hemming, "although it was quite possible for them to change direction, to be diverted to a different purpose while on the march."

One of those easily diverted was Vasco Núñez de Balboa.

The Search for Dabeiba

The first permanent Spanish town established

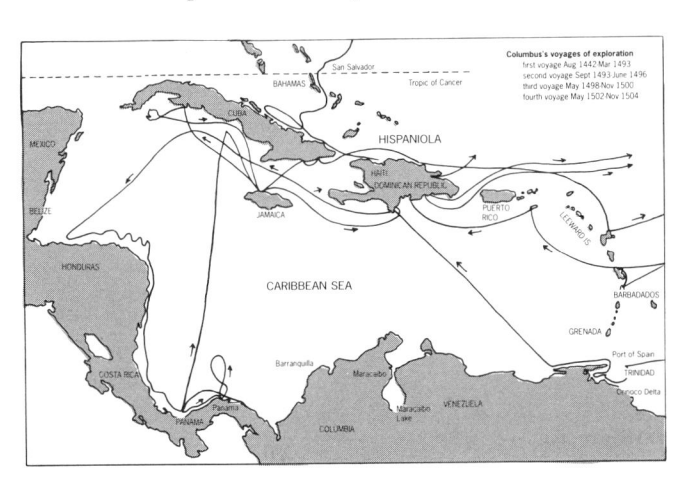

Despite three voyages to the New World, Columbus never found the rich source of gold he believed was there.

Vasco Núñez de Balboa

in the New World was Santa Maria la Antigua de Darien, later shortened to Darien. It was located close to the border of what later became Panama, a part of Central America. In 1512, Vasco Núñez de Balboa, a Spanish explorer, left the town of Darien with an expedition bent on reaching the territory of a chieftain named Dabeiba. This cacique lived in the mountainous interior to the south. According to the natives on the coast, he provided all the gold that reached the Gulf of Uraba where Darien was built.

Balboa explored the Rio Atrato and the rivers that flowed into it, but when he was only two days' journey from the land of Dabeiba he turned back. It is not clear why, but some clues may be found in a letter he wrote to King Ferdinand II. It said in part:

> Many Indians who have seen it tell me that this cacique Dabeiba has certain baskets of gold, and that it requires the whole strength of a man to lift one of these onto his shoulders. This cacique gets the gold from some distance away, in the mountains, and the manner by which he gets it is thus: two days' journey away, there is a beautiful land where the people are very Carib and bad. They eat as many humans as they can get.... They are the owners of these mines, which, according to the news I have heard, are the richest in the world.... There are two methods of collecting the gold, without any effort. One is to wait until the streams have risen in the ravines, and then, when the floods have passed and the river beds are dry again, the gold is exposed, having been washed out from the banks and carried from the mountains in very sizeable nuggets.... Another way of collecting gold is to await the time when the vegetation has dried in the mountains, and then to set it on fire. After the burning, they go and look in the heights and in the most likely places, and they collect it in great quantity and in fine nuggets. The Indians who collect this

Balboa and his crew received generous gifts of gold and emeralds from the South American natives.

gold, bring it in grains, just as they find it, in order to have it melted, and they trade it with this cacique Dabeiba.

In exchange he gives them boys and girls to eat, and women to serve them as wives, whom they do not eat. He also gives them peccaries [a kind of pig], of which there are many in this land, and much fish, cotton cloth, and salt, and also such objects of worked gold as they desire. These Indians trade only with the cacique Dabeiba, and nowhere else.... This cacique Dabeiba has a great place for melting gold in his house, and he has a hundred men continuously working gold.

With information such as this it is easy to see why Balboa wanted to find the land of Dabeiba. But if those who owned the rivers and the fields where the gold was found ate boys and girls, would they also eat foreign explorers who came uninvited into their territory? It may have been a chance that this Spanish expedition did not want to take.

The Discovery of the Pacific Ocean

History shows that Balboa, though he led

Balboa and other explorers had to face many difficulties in the new land. Among the scariest were the tribes of cannibals that supposedly inhabited the jungles.

Although Balboa did not discover a source of gold, he found something perhaps more valuable: He discovered the Pacific Ocean and claimed it in the name of the Kingdom of Spain.

other exploratory expeditions, bypassed Dabeiba's land. In 1513 he led an exploratory party to the shores of the Pacific Ocean. In a formal ceremony he claimed the ocean and all the lands in it as property of the Spanish monarchs.

All of Spain was excited by Balboa's discovery! Explorers who had lost interest in finding a waterway to the East were inspired anew to seek a passage from the Caribbean Sea to the Pacific Ocean. It would be only a matter of time, they thought, until a waterway would be found. Missionaries, bent on converting the natives to Christianity, packed their bags and boarded ships. No one seemed deterred by the letter from Balboa describing the cannibals.

There were still plenty of gold-seekers, of course. And they did not all seek in South America. During these years there was scarcely any distinction in the European mind between Mexico, Central America, the islands of the West Indies, and the northern part of South America. Any gold that came from this entire area added fuel to the fire that was to become El Dorado. The story of the young Spaniard Hernando Cortéz became part of the saga.

Hernando Cortéz's Contribution

When Hernando Cortéz arrived in Mexico in 1519, he learned of the Aztec Indian empire. Its ruler, Montezuma, it was said, had pierced "the gristle of his nostriles, hanging thereat a rich emerald." Cortéz must have been fascinated at the prospect of meeting such a cacique! He was in luck, for Teuhtlilli, a representative of Montezuma, met Cortéz's party on the beach. Teuhtlilli presented Cortéz with food and gifts of jewels and gold. In return Cortéz politely gave the messenger glass beads, a carved armchair for Montezuma, and a medal with the figure of St. George on horseback slaying a dragon. The

The Spanish explorer Hernando Cortéz meets Montezuma, the chief of the Aztecs.

Aztecs took the gifts, but asked for a soldier's helmet. It seemed like an odd request, but the helmet was given.

In about a week, Teuhtlilli returned to the camp of Cortéz. With him were more than a hundred men. These men carried more gifts for the visitors. Among the gifts were:

...a wheel like a sun, as big as a cartwheel, with many sorts of pictures on it...the whole of fine gold....another wheel...of greater size made of silver of great brilliancy in imitation of the moon with other figures shown on it....and the chief brought back the helmet full of fine grains of gold.

So wrote Bernal Diaz del Castillo, in *The Discovery and Conquest of Mexico*. And this was not all. "Next came twenty golden ducks, of fine workmanship, some ornaments in the shape of their native dogs, many others in the shapes of tigers, lions, and monkeys, ten necklaces of very fine workmanship, some pendants. They brought crests of gold, plumes of rich, green feathers, silver crests...[and] models of deer in hollow gold."

But it was the soldier's helmet filled with un-

Golden fish hooks from pre-Columbian South America. If the natives could make even everyday tools like these from gold, how vast must their treasure have been?

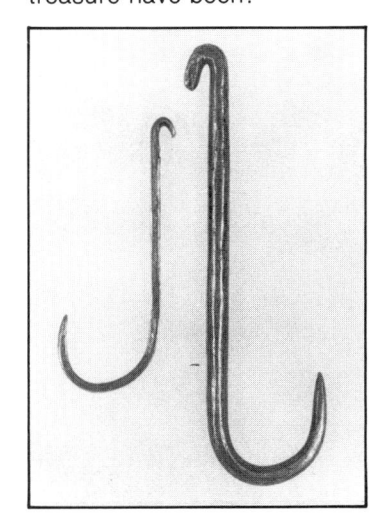

> "The conquistadores set their compass by rumors and myths passed on to them by tribes captured along their route. Often, the Indians were so terrorized that they lied about faraway treasures just to rid themselves of the Spaniards."
>
> Jonathan Kandell, *Passage Through El Dorado*

> "The prime mover of the Spaniards in their extraordinary adventures was not a thirst for gold, as is so often asserted, but a love of glory and a sense of patriotism."
>
> H. J. Mozans, *The Quest of El Dorado*

worked gold that brought the greatest response from Cortéz. He was interested in more than golden gifts. Like others before and after him, he wanted the *source* of the treasure. He reasoned that if these people had free gold in such quantity they had to have gold mines.

Yet, though Cortéz explored lower California and the Pacific coasts of Mexico, he found no mines. The gold he had received as gifts was sent home to Spain, and excitement reigned. Word spread that the New World was so rich that gold was used not only for ornaments, but for ordinary tools. Author Victor von Hagen says, "The fact that some barbarous people beyond the sea—of whom they had never previously heard—owned gold in such abundance that they could make golden fishhooks, prepared the public to accept the idea of golden cities in the New World."

Cortéz's letters were published in Nuremberg, Germany, where the Welser Company was located. This company was engaged in overseas trade. It acquired ginger, pepper, nutmeg, cinnamon, and cloves in Ceylon and India, and linen, cotton, silk, wool, and velvets from wherever it could get them. Until the arrival of Cortéz's Mexican gold, the Welsers' chief interest in the New World had been the bark of a certain guaiacum tree. This tree grew in the West Indies, and its hard brownish-green wood was used by the native people to cure disease.

The Welser Company, which was extremely successful, developed a considerable trade in this "medicine." Anton Welser has been portrayed in his counting rooms with a gold chain about his neck, counting his golden ducats (coins). It happened that the Welsers lent 141,000 of these ducats to Charles V, King of Spain, and Holy Roman Emperor. In turn, Charles gave the Welsers the governorship of the recently discovered territory of Venezuela. This entitled them to conquer and populate lands in the New World. As with other expeditions sponsored by Spanish royalty, the company was to give a fifth of all its profits to the king. "It was," says von Hagen, "the beginning of another 'journey to the Golden Man.'"

Ambitious Ambrosius Dalfinger

At the head of this expedition was Ambrosius Dalfinger, young, capable, and energetic. He was anxious to see what King Ferdinand had referred to as Castilla del Oro (Golden Castille). Dalfinger had no idea of the vastness of the land which lay before him. In 1529, the year he started out, the Spaniards' knowledge of the inland geography of South America was still vague. Far to the west lay the Andes Mountains, but a system of mountain ranges called the cordillera branched off from them. These mountains extend to the very edge and length of the Caribbean Sea. Their peaks rise to over sixteen thousand feet, so they are snow-capped most of the year. The lower parts of the mountains break up into sweeping plains of open

Charles V of Spain borrowed money from the Welser Company. In repayment, he gave the Welsers governorship of Venezuela.

This illustration from the sixteenth century is one of the only remaining paintings done of the conquistadores in their own time. It shows the leaders of the 1534 Welser expedition, marching toward their ships in a Spanish harbor. The three leaders are Georg Hohermuth, Nicolaus Federmann, and Andreas Gundelfiner.

Hieronymus Köler, another painter who never actually went to the New World, imaginatively—and not completely accurately (he shows the Indians with beards)—depicted a battle between Spaniards and Indians.

grasslands, and where there is water, these become jungle. The whole region was inhabited by a variety of tribes, most of them in constant war with each other.

If Dalfinger had known of the Indians' six-foot-long poisoned arrows he might not have been so eager to proceed. But proceed he did. Right into Jirajara country where he clashed immediately with these belligerent people. The Jirajara harrassed Ambrosius Dalfinger's small army most of the way through their territory. "But sometimes the wars would break off for trading," writes Victor von Hagen. "Ambrosius' men [offered] hawk's bells, knives, scissors, and other products of Ulm [Germany] in exchange for food." But the Indians did not have enough food to feed the army, and the expedition suffered terribly from hunger.

Esteban Martin, interpreter and journal keeper for the trip, wrote that the diet at times consisted of the hearts of chonta plants and the large grubs of giant beetles that lived within the palm trunks. Martin said they could, of course, "eat the tails of crocodiles and iguanas which, when skinned and prepared, were edible."

A Difficult Expedition

Dalfinger and his men were gone for eight months. The farthest west they got was Maracaibo. But they did manage to bring back some gold which they acquired from chieftains they met wearing gold earrings and crowns. It came to seven thousand pesos worth, which would be well over one hundred pounds of high-carat metal.

Despite intensive inquiries as to its origin, the conquistadores were only able to learn that the gold came from a people in the high interior who traded for raw cotton, coral, pearls, and the great strombus shells used "to call down the gods." These people of the interior also were rich in green stones. But Dalfinger's army was in no shape to go looking for this tribe. "Almost all [the survivors of the expedition] were half-dead," reports von Hagen, "including Dalfinger himself—fevered, emaciated and hanging on to life only by the call of some golden siren voice."

It must have been a very strong voice, for Dalfinger went on a second expedition in 1531. He left Coro, Venezuela, to strike south this time. Again he had Esteban Martin along to write reports of the expedition. As they marched across the coastal plain behind the Guajira peninsula, they passed across the territories of successive tribes. Some were "very domestic and unwarlike." But these peaceful tribes were wary of the explorers. They had learned that visitors not only traded, but often killed by brutal means. Dalfinger's group proved to be no exception. "We made peace with them, but they did not trust us much," wrote Martin. As the expedition headed inland, the Indians they met either fled or tried to make peace with small offerings of gold.

One tribe, the Pacabueyes, was the sort of

"Every expedition was an absolute failure.... [El Dorado] was as unattainable as the flitting rainbow."

H. J. Mozans, *The Quest of El Dorado*

"The legend of the Golden Man inspired more sustained exploration, of some of the wildest parts of South America, than any comparable idea, anywhere else in the world."

John Hemming, *The Search for El Dorado*

A European artist imagined a sophisticated Indian gold refinery.

tribe that all conquistadores hoped to find, according to author John Hemming. They "welcomed strangers: ten or twelve villages came in peace." From these tribes, Dalfinger recruited porters for the expedition's gear. The army rested for a time at a village called Pauxoto and then moved on thirty miles to Tomara, a town of over a thousand huts. Esteban Martin wrote glowingly of this area:

> This town is the best we had seen in that entire land. It is on a height and very airy, with many savannahs and small hillocks.... There is plenty of game, deer, partridges and iguanas.

"But the greatest attraction of the Pacabueyes was their gold," says Hemming. Martin wrote, "In some eight days we obtained, by gifts or by raiding, over 20,000 castellanos [approximately two hundred pounds].... All the Indians of this town of Tomara work gold. They have their forges and anvils, little hammers, and scales with which they weigh gold."

The conquistadores left a horrifying history of abuse of the Indians behind them. They killed and enslaved the native people and forcefully converted them to Christianity.

Treasure Hunt and Bloodbath

What had started out as a trip to see what lay beyond Lake Maracaibo turned out to be a successful treasure hunt. Successful, at least, for the explorers.

For the tribes of the area, it was "a bloodbath," reports John Hemming. "Dalfinger's expedition was notorious for keeping its native porters chained at the neck in a train of human misery. If one person flagged or died, it was customary to behead the corpse so that the body fell and there was no need to undo the shackle." The army moved from one village to another, destroying and ravaging with bloodthirsty fury, even burning chiefs.

"Had the expedition made peaceful contact or interrogated captives," says Hemming, "it might have learned that [at one point] it was only a few days' march from the northern edge of the territory of the Muiscas—the Chibcha people whose wealth was to inspire part of the El Dorado legend." But Dalfinger's men suspected nothing

On occasion, the natives took revenge on the brutal conquistadores. One method of punishment was to pour molten gold down the throats of the greedy Europeans.

of this. Of course they had not yet heard of the Golden Man; their quest was for a golden land that would bring them riches and fame.

Dalfinger spent some months among the Pacabueyes, leading small expeditions into the interior, returning to the main group periodically. On one of these expeditions he was hit on the neck with a poison arrow. Author Hemming says Dalfinger survived for only four days before dying "delirious and raving from the poison in the deserted village of the tribe that killed him."

A Treasure Lost

At one point in the expedition a Lieutenant Iñigo de Vascuña was sent back to Coro with the gold the army had been gathering. The group under his command lost its way. Hemming recounts their horrifying story using quotes from Francisco Martin:

> They divided the gold among them, with each... carrying ten to twelve pounds. Having no food, they were reduced to eating bitter palm hearts, so tough that they broke their swords on them. They were growing weaker, hungry, and often barefoot or lame. They came to a broad river and attempted to descend it in rafts, but one of the rafts capsized with its load of gold. Some men pushed ahead on land, but one group tried to remain on a raft; they were found next day riddled with arrows.... The men [who were left] had by now eaten their horses and a dog. "They were very exhausted and starving, cutting a path with pieces of their swords, most of which were broken."

Some of the men wanted to leave the gold, which was becoming an intolerable burden. But Vascuña persuaded them to stagger on for a further week. In the end they were forced to leave their beloved gold, burying it in a basket beneath a tree and blazing all the surrounding trees with their swords.

This account came to light only after Francisco Martin, the sole survivor of the twenty-five

The luckless Spaniards who were hit by the poisoned arrows of Amazonian natives did not live to spend the profits of their travels.

men sent back to Coro, was picked up in the jungle. He had been abandoned by Vascuña's expedition when his feet were eaten by worms. Some Indians had found him and tended him. For a year he had lived among them as an Indian.

Francisco added an enticing bit of information: The gold had been buried not only once—but twice. The dying men were so obsessed with their gold that they used their remaining strength to dig up the treasure and rebury it under a towering tree beside a creek. Hemming continues the story: "An expedition naturally set off the following year taking Francisco Martin to try to locate the tree under which Vascuña's men had buried their gold. It was never found by those or later seekers. It is presumably still there, somewhere between the Catatumbo and Santa Ana rivers to the west of Lake Maracaibo."

The Gold of the Incas

The next conquistadore to have a golden dream was on his way into the interior while Dalfinger was still in the wilderness. His name was Francisco Pizarro, and he had been given a license to conquer a land to the southwest. This was the territory of the Inca Indians.

The realm of the Incas stretched across parts of what are now four nations: Ecuador, Peru, Bolivia, and Chile. The Spanish had known of the existence of the Inca Empire and of its golden wealth for five years, since they had made exploratory voyages southward along the Ecuadorian and Peruvian coastline. Now they returned, intent on conquest. Their leader was Francisco Pizarro. John Man, in *The Kings of Eldorado*, writes that Pizarro was "a determined, experienced, and dauntless commander." And he was highly successful.

With one hundred seventy men he marched down the coast of Peru and into the mountains.

"There are times when it would have been far better if a treasure had never been found. For all the riches involved, no good came of it."

Alvin Schwartz, *Gold & Silver, Silver & Gold*

"The adventurers who went in quest of El Dorado...contributed greatly to the advancement of geographic knowledge and to the progress of civilization."

H. J. Mozans, *The Quest of El Dorado*

Francisco Pizarro, one of three Pizarro brothers who sought their fortunes in the New World.

There, in 1532, he captured the Inca leader, Atahualpa. It must have seemed that even the greed of the most ambitious conquistadore was about to be satisfied. The Inca bargained for his life by promising to fill the room in which he was being held to a height of eight feet with precious objects of gold. In addition Atahualpa offered Pizarro twice that amount of silver.

From throughout the empire, gold and silver objects came trickling in from Atahualpa's loyal subjects. But apparently the ransom did not come fast enough for the impatient Spaniards. They overran Cuzco, the capital city of the Incas where the Temple of the Sun was located. From this square structure of stone, about two hundred feet long, they pried seven hundred golden plates which sheathed the walls.

Cuzco, with its temple of gold, could easily be

Chief Atahualpa's subjects brought all kinds of gold objects to Pizarro in hope of ransoming their leader.

Despite the treasures the Indians offered, Pizarro's men killed Atahualpa.

called a city of gold. The finding of rich cities such as this only added to the Spaniards' belief that more golden cities were to be found.

Pizarro and his men did not release the emperor from captivity, in spite of the ransom they collected, but strangled him with an iron collar. Then they looted and pillaged their way southward. Part of the expedition left the larger group to pursue a band of natives they thought had taken some of Atahualpa's gold and fled with it to the east.

On to Bolivia

In the basin of the Amazon River, which begins in the Andes Mountains, the great empire of Pay-titi the "Tiger Father" was said to be still

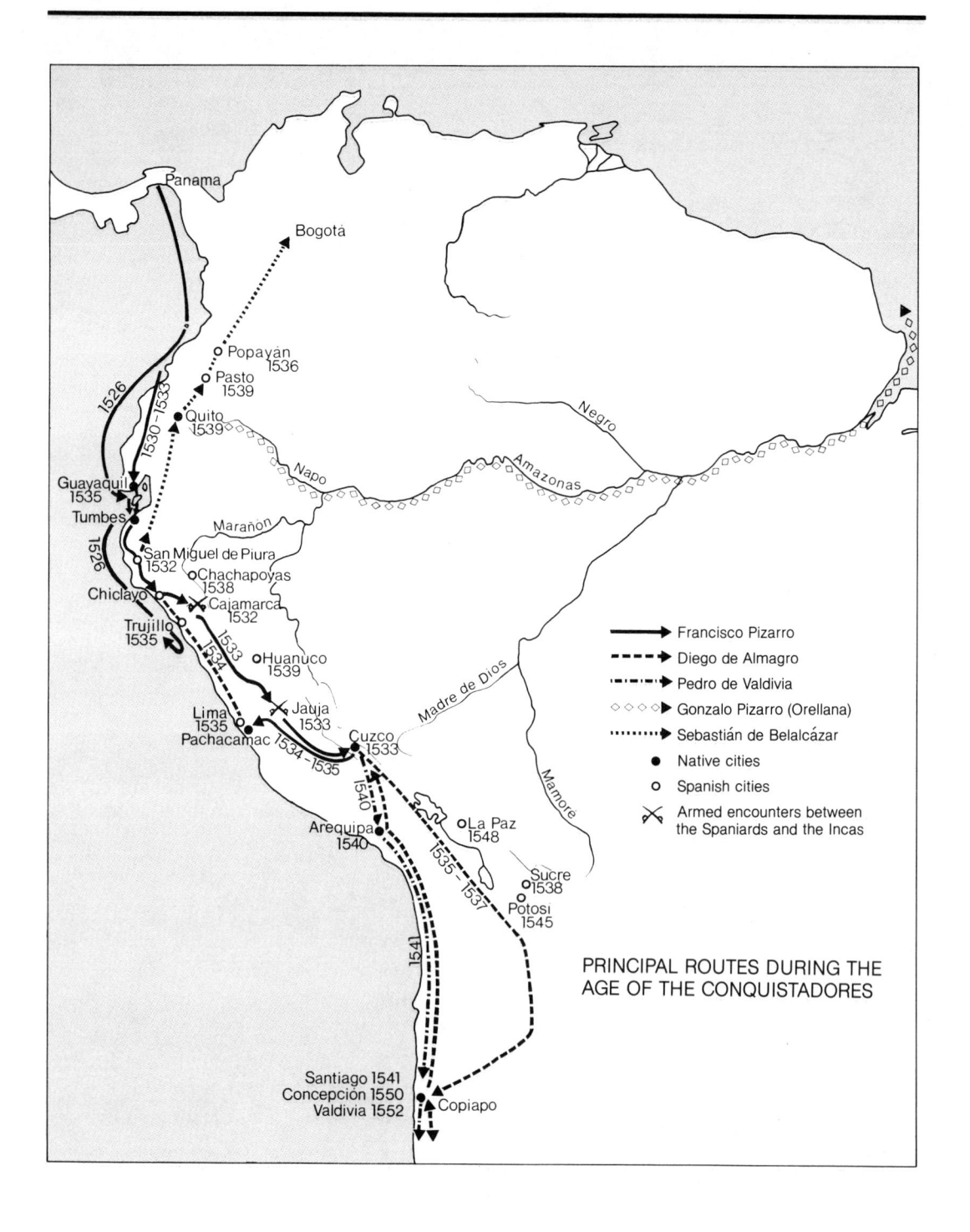

PRINCIPAL ROUTES DURING THE AGE OF THE CONQUISTADORES

flourishing. The Spanish set their compasses "by rumors and myths passed on to them by tribes captured along their route," according to Jonathan Kandell, in *Passage Through El Dorado*. Kandell quotes Father José Guevara, an eighteenth-century historian:

> The Paititi [his spelling] is an extremely rich kingdom. This kingdom is isolated in the middle of a great lagoon surrounded by mountains of untold riches. Its buildings are all of white stone, and has avenues, piazas and temples. From the center of the lagoon, the palace of the emperor Mojos rises, superior to all the other structures in size, beauty and wealth, its doors chained in gold.

But "the conquistadores found not a trace of Pay-titi in [Bolivia]. Cursing the warlike tribes and the absence of treasure, they moved on," writes Kandell.

Kandell believes that the Indian legends of a rich kingdom may have come from this and other stories of cities secluded in the mountains. In many cases the city described was built in the center of a lake, or on its shores.

Whatever the case, the hunt for a golden city, richer than any found so far, had been going on for four decades. The name El Dorado had not yet been given to this elusive kingdom. But the hope of finding such a place was already a reality.

Did it exist somewhere?

The Peruvian natives seemed genuinely convinced of the existence of a rich kingdom somewhere in their vicinity. But then so did the natives to the north. Could all these tribes be telling the truth, or did they generously point out the way to a golden land just to rid themselves of the marauding Europeans?

Opposite: This map shows the routes of several of the conquistadores who sought golden cities.

Three

A Legend Takes Shape

The treasure hunt that had started in the islands of the Caribbean and spread to Mexico gained momentum with Pizarro's looting of Peru. It next became concentrated in what is now the South American country of Colombia. Rumors of a Golden Man inspired the search anew.

A Messenger from the Northeast

Author Timothy Severin says that a few months after the fall of the Inca empire in 1532, an Indian messenger from a then-unknown tribe appeared in Peru from the northeast. He came in search of Atahualpa. Not knowing that the Inca chief had been overthrown, the messenger walked straight into the hands of the Spaniards. They interrogated him about his mission, and he revealed that he had been sent by the Zipa, a ruling lord of Bogotá in Colombia. Asked to describe his homeland, the messenger told of a splendid capital city, far away, where a priest-king, covered in gold, dived into a lake surrounded by high mountains.

"The legend of El Dorado had finally come to the ears of Europeans," says Severin.

"It was a beguiling story," says author John Hemming, "and it quickly caught the imagination of the conquistadores. It...gained credibility, and evolved in detail during the ensuing century."

But was it true? Was there a Golden Man, or a golden city?

Opposite: One of the treasures found in the land of El Dorado. This "golden man" wears a nose ornament similar to those worn by many people in the Sinú tribe.

41

Myth or Reality?

Timothy Severin leads his readers to believe the original story of the ceremony at Lake Guatavita was based on fact, but John Hemming thinks otherwise. He says the whole idea of El Dorado may be "one of the most famous chimeras [imaginary monsters made up of many parts] in history...that lured hundreds of hard men into desperate expeditions." Other writers contribute other opinions.

Demetrio Ramos Perez, a distinguished Venezuelan historian, traced the beginning of the legend through documented sources. His painstaking research led him to conclude that it was entirely unconnected with the Chibcha (also known as the Muisca) Indians, located near Lake Guatavita. Perez dismissed the golden man as an attractive story.

Fernández de Oviedo, however, approached the possibility with a more open mind. De Oviedo had been on many expeditions, and he based his opinions on his experiences. In addition, he interviewed others who had returned from the interior. De Oviedo wrote:

> I asked Spaniards who have been in Quito...why they call that prince [of whom they spoke] the "Golden Chief or King." They tell me that what they have learned from the Indians is that that great lord or prince goes about continually covered in gold dust as fine as ground salt. He feels that it would be less beautiful to wear any other ornament. It would be crude and common to put on armour plates of hammered or stamped gold, for other rich lords wear these when they wish. But to powder oneself with gold is something exotic, unusual, novel and more costly—for he washes away at night what he puts on each morning, so that it is discarded and lost, and he does this every day of the year. With this custom, going about clothed and covered in that way, he

An eighteenth-century Dutch engraving depicts the gilding of El Dorado.

has no impediment or hindrance. The fine proportions of his body and natural form, on which he prides himself, are not covered or obscured, for he wears no other clothing of any sort on top of it.

Here, then, was a gilded man who wore gold as everyday clothing. De Oviedo went on to explain just how this rich ruler managed to do this.

> He anoints himself every morning with a certain gum or resin that sticks very well. The powdered gold adheres to that unction...until his entire body is covered from the soles of his feet to his head. He looks as resplendent as a gold object worked by the hand of a great artist. I believe that, if that chief does do this, he must have very rich mines of fine quality gold. On the Mainland, I have in fact seen plenty of the gold that Spaniards call placer gold [particles], in such quantities that he could easily do what is said.

De Oviedo seemed a bit skeptical, but he did not regard El Dorado as pure fantasy. The Spaniards who talked to de Oviedo about the Golden Man may have based their stories on actual Indian customs.

Painted Bodies

Members of many American Indian tribes paint their bodies for special ceremonies. But a Jesuit priest named José Gumilla who lived among the tribes of the Orinoco Valley in South America in the seventeenth century observed that

> With very few exceptions, all tribes of those lands anoint themselves from the crowns of their heads to the tips of their feet with oil and achote. Mothers anoint all their children, even those at the breast, at the same time as they anoint themselves, at least twice a day in the morning and at nightfall. They later anoint their husbands very liberally. On special days a great variety of drawings in different colours goes on top of the unction....The ordinary daily unction is a mix-

---

"Sometimes, the Indians...repeated legends of civilizations that may once have existed but had died out long before the arrival of the conquistadores."

Jonathan Kandell, *Passage Through El Dorado*

"Contemporary sources leave no doubt that [the idea of El Dorado as a place]...was the creation of the Spaniards themselves."

John Hemming, *The Search for El Dorado*

Many South American natives painted their bodies with colored clays and oils. This practice encouraged the conquistadores' belief that the Indians may have used gold in the same way.

ture of oil and anatto that we call achote. It is ground and kneaded with oil of cunáma or turtle eggs. It serves not only as clothing but as a sure defence against mosquitoes, which abound in such a great number of species. It not only prevents mosquitos from biting them, but the insects stick in the gum.

Hemming adds that this coating is also cool, a protection against the heat of the sun. "Amazon tribes still do this regularly," he says, "painting their bodies with scarlet anatto or black genipapo vegetable dyes."

If naked tribes painted themselves red or black, why not gold also?

Warwick Bray in his book, *The Gold of El Dorado*, writes that, "There were Indians still alive who had witnessed the last Guatavita ceremony, and the stories these Indians told were consistent. Every one of the Spanish chroniclers refers to the Gilded Man."

But Hemming says only a few authors were the "primary sources for the original El Dorado legend. All later writers embellished these early accounts."

Juan Rodriguez Freyle's version of the Golden Man story however, seemed to have some degree of authority. He said he learned of El Dorado "from a friend, Don Juan, nephew of the last independent lord of Guatavita." Freyle's account was written in 1636. He said the ceremony took place not as a rite of spring, but on the appointment of a new ruler, or Zipa. Before taking office, the new chief spent some time secluded in a cave, without women, forbidden to eat salt and chili pepper, or to go out during daylight. The rest of the account is much the same as the other versions, with the sacrifices of gold being placed on a raft and dropped into the lake amid the playing of musical instruments, and the raft returning to shore where singing and dancing took place. Freyle said, "With this ceremony the new ruler was received, and was recognized as lord and king. From this ceremony came the celebrated name of El Dorado."

Could a story repeated so many times with so few variations be completely false?

And if there was a Golden Man, why not a golden city? Even a golden kingdom.

Lake Guatavita, where many explorers believed the ceremony of the Golden Man originated. The large notch on the far shore was caused by a sixteenth-century attempt to drain the lake to find gold.

If El Dorado existed, where was it? During the last four centuries, many people have tentatively identified it, but no one has actually found it. This map shows several possible locations.

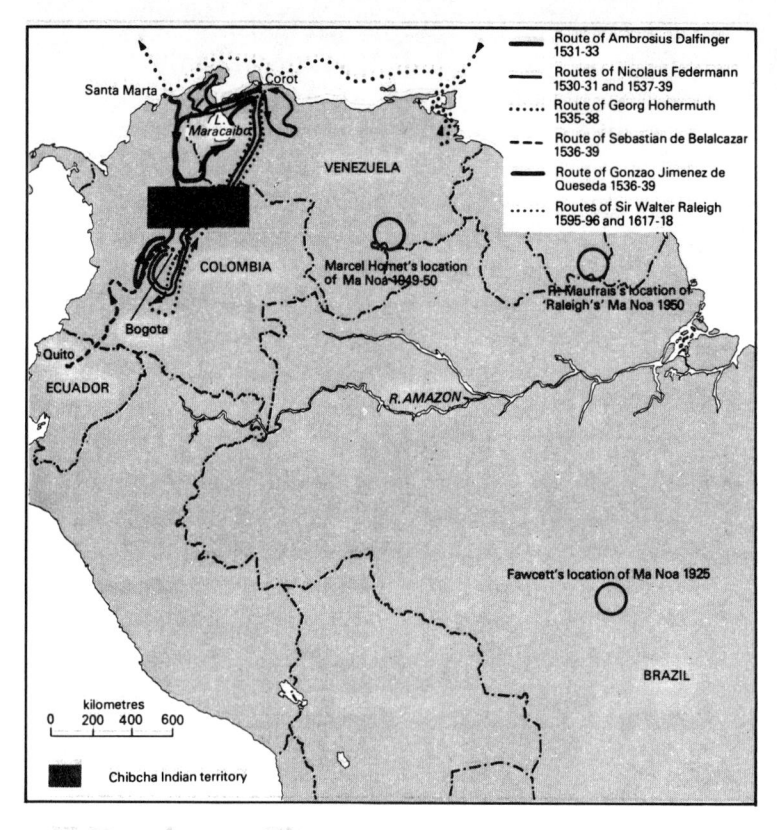

El Dorado as a Place

Author John Hemming tried to trace the origin of the concept of El Dorado as a place. He states: "All sources show that it started in Quito; and contemporary sources leave no doubt that it took shape there in late 1540."

The story was brought back by men returning from fighting with the Yalcones Indians at the settlement of Timana. Hemming says the Spaniards became convinced that the Indians were defending Timana so fiercely because it was the gateway to greater riches. One of the men who had been on that expedition said the army had only *begun* to find some rich settlements.

John Hemming goes on to say that, "The idea of gold dust so fine that it could be anointed like the dyes used by the Orinoco Indians, seems to have combined with earlier notions that the rich lands should be sought 'behind the mountains' and in the gold-bearing lands close to the equator. The region east of Quito or south of Timana would fit this location."

As additional evidence, a report by an unknown writer in 1541 stated:

> From the province of Timana to the province of El Dorado, which...is considered a rich affair, there are about 36 leagues (over one hundred miles)....[El Dorado] has a large lake with certain islands...and appears [to be] on the equator or very close to it.

Another writer, Pedro de Cieza de León, a soldier-historian, passed through Quito in 1540. Later he wrote that Gonzalo Pizarro, youngest brother of Francisco, was "eager to discover the valley of El Dorado." This land, it was said, lay beyond the mountains east of Quito. An expedition had just returned from an attempt to find cinnamon in those wild hills. The members of the expedition reported that "the Indians said that further on, if they advanced, they would come to a wide-spreading flat country, teeming with Indians who possess great riches, for they all wear gold ornaments, and where there are no forests nor mountain ranges. When this news spread in Quito, everyone there wanted to take part in the expedition."

Gonzalo Pizarro himself wrote to the king,
> Because of many reports which I received in Quito and outside that city, from prominent and very aged chiefs as well as from Spaniards, whose accounts agreed with one another, that the province of La Canela [Cinnamon] and Lake El Dorado were a very populous and very rich land, I decided to go and conquer and explore it.

With this letter, El Dorado became associated with spices as well as other treasures.

"City, personage, or kingdom, [El Dorado] always lay beyond the next range of mountains, or deep in the unexplored forests."

Warwick Bray, *The Gold of El Dorado*

"They were searching for something that did not exist."

Caspar Montibelli, *The World's Last Mysteries*

Above is pictured the Atacama Desert, a site of a major salt mine. Jiménez de Quesada was seeking gold as well as salt, a valued commodity in Europe.

But what was El Dorado, exactly? A Golden Man, a city of gold, or a lake?

Spices and Gold

Those who wrote of spices and lakes contributed to—or perhaps merely confused—the story.

Jiménez de Quesada, another conquistadore, who wrote about lakes, connected El Dorado with salt, almost as valuable as cinnamon. On his journey up from the Magdalena valley, Quesada thought his men would find a lake that produced the salt cakes traded by the Muisca Indians. He said this was "the lake of the salt, in which, as they were assured by the Indians, there was a very large town of many huts and many golden effigies [images of persons]."

There *were* many lakes in Muisca territory, as well as large towns and gold objects. Quesada said that the Muisca "have many woods and lakes consecrated to their false religion. . . . They also go to do their sacrifices in these woods and they bury gold and emeralds in them. . . . They do the same in the lakes which they have dedicated for their sacrifices. They go there and throw in much gold and precious stones, which are thus lost forever."

Information such as this led those who came later to look for treasure not only in Lake Guatavita, but in other lakes as well.

It seems that if one were going to look for El Dorado, the place to start would be somewhere between Quito and Bogotá, to the north. Or would it?

An eighteenth-century author, Basilio Vicente de Oviedo, located El Dorado on the Ariari River, near the Orinoco, farther to the northeast. Here, he wrote, was "a land so rich that tufts of grass pulled from the ground had gold dust on their roots." Every year a young man of the local tribe

One tribe was said to sacrifice young men by cutting them open and "salting" them with gold.

was chosen by lot and offered as a sacrifice to the tribe's idol. "They open him up and salt him with gold dust, and offer him as a sacrifice in their church. Because of this they call him El Dorado."

Growth of the Legend

Thus the legend of El Dorado evolved from many sources: from a vague notion of a rich, flat land east of Quito, from Fernández de Oviedo's story of a prince anointed daily, from Juan Rodriguez Freyle's account of the installation of a new ruler, and from Basilio Vicente de Oviedo's description of ritual human sacrifice.

Which version is true? All of them have some things in common: a lake, the use of gold dust in sacrificial ceremonies, and rich rulers.

El Dorado became much larger than a single ceremony at Lake Guatavita. It became the inspiration that pulled flagging explorers deeper into the interior of South America.

Four

The Dream Becomes an Obsession

Opposite: Those seeking the gold of El Dorado were faced with many natural obstacles, including never-ending jungle, strange and dangerous animals and insects, and imposing natural features such as this high stone bridge.

The dreams of gold that led to the early exploration of the New World were nothing compared to the gold fever that gripped those who now heard of El Dorado. His kingdom was their goal—the pot of gold at the end of the rainbow. The search was a race. Who would win? Who would find the golden city?

The Man Who Coined the Term

Sebastian de Belalcázar was a member of Francisco Pizarro's expedition that conquered Atahualpa in Peru. A trusted soldier, Belalcázar was sent back to the port of San Miguel de Piera with some of the enormous treasure from Peru. His share was a sizable fortune in silver and gold, enough so that he could have retired in comfort. But while he was on the coast, Belalcázar was convinced by some adventurers that there was more gold to be found to the north. He started a treasure hunt of his own.

Belalcázar followed a fine road the Incas had built through the valleys of the Andes mountains. His immediate goal was to overtake Runiñaui, a one-eyed general of Atahualpa's who had evaded capture and fled with remnants of his army.

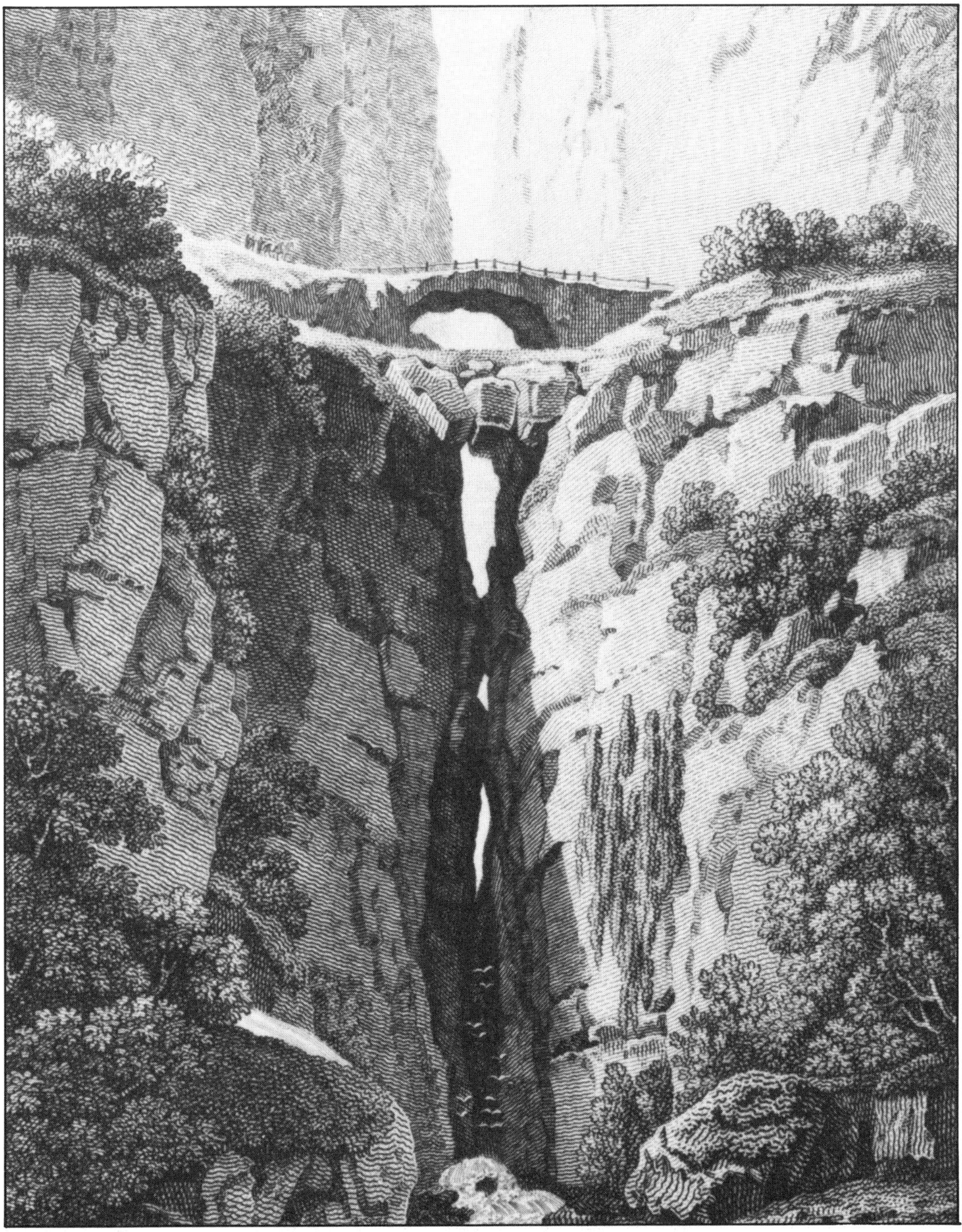

Sebastian de Belalcázar first explored with Francisco Pizarro. Later he went on expeditions of his own, seeking more gold and other valuables.

"Belalcázar," writes author John Hemming, "was convinced that they had hidden Atahualpa's gold." When he found the Inca general and his men, Belalcázar defeated the last of Atahualpa's forces. All the Inca chiefs were tortured, but they "behaved with great composure and left him with nothing but his greed." Belalcázar claimed the city of Quito in 1534, declaring it to be Spanish territory.

The details of what happened next vary by account. Most historians agree that Belalcázar first heard of a gilded man in 1536 when he was preparing for a second expedition. According to John Hemming, one of Belalcázar's officers captured a native chief who the Spaniards knew as *el indio dorado*—the golden Indian. Author von Hagen states that Belalcázar dubbed this Indian *El Dorado* after hearing from him the story of the king who was coated in gold dust and performed ceremonies in a lake. This king, said the Indian, lived twelve days north of Quito, and was "as resplendent as the beaming sun."

Whether Belalcázar actually coined the phrase "El Dorado" is not known, but his expedition led to a strange meeting in the interior of South America.

Belalcázar started off on his second expedition, leaving a lieutenant in charge in Quito. Apparently he was in no hurry, and since he intended to start new cities, he took along giant mastiff dogs, cattle, horses, hosts of Indians, and a huge herd of swine and pregnant sows. "Progress," reports von Hagen, "was thus pig-paced."

He made progress enough, for in 1537 he founded the cities of Popayan and Cali. In July 1538 he, along with two hundred men, discovered the sources of the upper Magdalena river. He did this despite the fact that he lost twenty of his troops to attacks by Indians armed with poisoned arrows. Pedro de Cieza recalled the episode: "With poison on the arrows it was only necessary to make a skin prick and bring out a drop of blood when quickly the poison (curare) reached the heart. The victim, overcome by nausea, bites his own hand and begs quickly for death."

Even so, when Belalcázar's forces reached the land of the Chibcha Indians on the plateau of Bogotá, they had fared very well. Belalcázar and his men were still wearing rich clothes of silk, fine cloaks, silver ornaments, and coats of mail. They still had many Indian servants and a great quantity of pigs to sustain them. Belalcázar learned that other Spaniards were in the area, and soon he met another expedition.

A Bedraggled and Hungry Group

In 1536, the same year Belalcázar heard of the Golden Man, Gonzalo Jiménez de Quesada began exploring to the south of Santa Marta on Colombia's northern coast. With nine hundred men he had struggled through forest so dense that it formed a living wall of vegetation, "and each step had to be carved out with machetes [large heavy knives] and then widened," according to Caspar Montibelli in *The World's Last Mysteries*. "Snakes and alligators were a constant peril, and the party was decimated by fever, malaria, and the attacks of hostile natives." The explorers were at the end of their strength when suddenly the countryside changed: They, too, had reached the land of the Chibcha Indians, a fertile plateau where maize (corn), beans, and nuts were cultivated. Quesada's men, now reduced to fewer than two hundred, entered this area.

In the village of Sogamoso they came upon a temple dedicated to the sun god. Inside were the mummified remains of numerous Chibcha kings. Emeralds filled their eye sockets and gold ornaments covered their bodies. The Chibchas

"All the vessels of [El Dorado's] home, table, and kitchen were of gold and silver.... He had statues of gold which seemed giants, and the figures...of all the beasts, birds, trees, and fishes that the sea or waters of his kingdom breedeth."

Francisco López de Gómara, sixteenth-century chronicler

"It makes an attractive story but has no factual basis."

Warwick Bray, *The Gold of El Dorado*

The dense rainforest formed "a living wall of vegetation" that the conquistadores often found almost impossible to cut through.

claimed that they had obtained the gold from another Indian tribe in exchange for bars of salt. They also told the Spaniards of a lake called Guatavita, a few days' march away. At Guatavita, so the story went, a strange annual ceremony took place—the ceremony of the Golden Man.

The Spaniards immediately set out for the lake with an Indian guide. Caspar Montibelli writes,

> They found it to be a deep, dark expanse of water set in the crater of an extinct volcano almost nine thousand feet above sea level. There were a few huts, but of the Golden Man and his people there was no sign. The treasure—if there was any—was on the bottom of the lake.

Quesada and his army set off again, hoping to find the golden king who was not at Guatavita.

But the rugged country had taken its toll, and by the time Quesada encountered Belalcázar, the contrast between the two forces was glaring. Three years had passed. Author von Hagen writes that "years in battle and terrifying travels had reduced Quesada's men to appear as mounted gypsies." Seeing that they were near starvation, Belalcázar treated the rival army to a feast! Instead of fighting, they discussed who had the right to this land.

All the while this drama was taking place, another expedition was approaching. It was in even worse shape than Quesada's group.

Enter Nicolaus Federmann

Like Ambrosius Dalfinger, Nicolaus Federmann was a German employed by the banking house of Welser. Federmann's force, numbering four hundred men, had set out from Coro on the Gulf of Venezuela. They had been roaming about the mountains for three and a half years when they appeared on the plateau with Quesada and Belalcázar.

Federmann's men were ill-fed and fever-stricken. They wore animal skins and their hair was long and loose "after the Indian style," says von Hagen. Their horses were so lean that ribs showed through the blankets on their backs. And the expedition had found nothing. Still, Federmann and his men felt that this land, which held the promise of El Dorado, lay under their jurisdiction. But so did the other armies gathered on the plateau.

Each of the armies now numbered exactly one hundred sixty six men, according to most sources. The fact that their forces were equal is as astounding as the coincidence of their meeting in the same place at the same time.

"The three captains warily greeted one another," writes Caspar Montibelli. "They eventually arrived at a gentleman's agreement." Quesada gave Federmann some forty pounds of gold and emeralds he had obtained from the

The native people of Peru, like those of many cultures, worshipped the life-giving sun.

Belalcázar's, Quesada's, and Federmann's troops met on a rainforest plateau where together they founded the city of Bogotá, Colombia. The contrast between the groups was amazing—from Belalcázar's silk-gowned and well-fed entourage to Federmann's scruffy, starving crew.

Gonzalo Jiménez de Quesada

Chibchas. Belalcázar, already rich, asked for no compensation. They agreed to let the Council of the Indies in Spain divide among them the governorships of the territories they had explored.

So it was, according to von Hagen, "On April 29, 1539, one of those rare sunlit unmisted days on the plain of Bogotá, that Quesada, Federmann and Belalcázar became the three founders of the city [of Bogotá]."

They had assured themselves a place in history, but none had achieved his goal of finding the kingdom of the gilded Indian. Belalcázar returned to his earlier conquests, and Federmann died in obscurity. Years later, Quesada mounted another expedition which lasted three years. It ended when he suffered a severe financial loss.

The Hazardous Jungle

Other adventurers continued the search for El Dorado. By 1541, the legend was well established. "El Dorado [was responsible for sending] men marching into the depths of South America. And their target area was the eastern foothills of the Andes, six hundred kilometers [372 miles] southwest of Bogotá—one of the wildest places in all the tough interior of South America," says John Hemming.

It took brave souls to plunge into such a wilderness. Expeditions had to make their way blindly through endless forest, never knowing what lay ahead, gauging the slope of the forest floor to find streams for drinking water. Author John Hemming tells in detail what this area is like:

> It is a dark world, dank with the smell of rotting leaves. Sometimes the forest opens into the gloomy majesty of a cathedral, with fallen trees lying like great tombs. In such places the going is easy and the danger is of losing direction—for the sun is visible only filtered through the canopy far

overhead, or striking down in rare shafts of blinding brilliance, with huge blue morpho butterflies hovering over the leaves that it illuminates on the forest floor. More often, the jungle is lower and denser. There are lush fans of spiny ferns and cascades of creepers, mosses and bryophytes [a nonflowering plant] hanging from the trees. Explorers have to hack a path through the foliage. Thin saplings can be severed easily with a blow from a machete, but creepers dance aside when struck and have to be pinned against a tree and chopped. The cutting seems easier in the morning, when machetes are sharp and cutting arms are rested; but by the afternoon, when it is hotter, it takes two or three frustrating blows to clear something that could have been cut with a sharp "ping" in the morning. The dead leaves seethe with ants, ticks and jiggers. There are swarms of biting blackfly...during the day, and mosquitoes at night. Men cutting trails must wear broad-rimmed hats, for a blow at a creeper will bring down a shower of insects, twigs, scorpions or tree snakes. The cutting might disturb a nest of fierce forest hornets. By the end of a few weeks of such toil, men are pale and thin, with their clothes torn and boots disintegrating.

Faced with such misery, it is a testimony to the

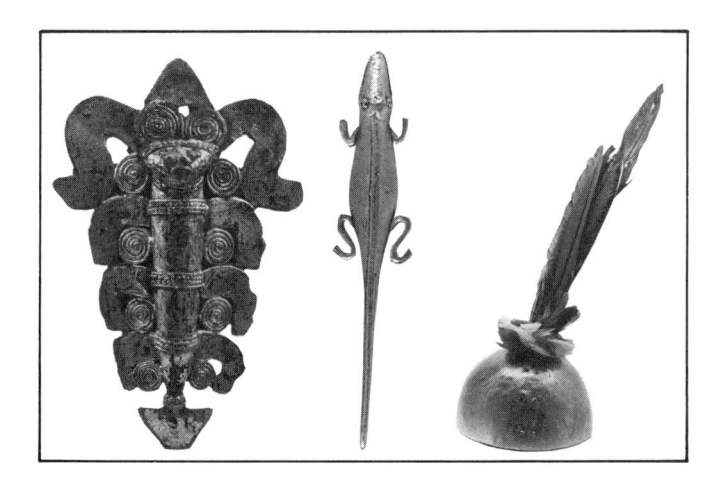

Despite the hardships, enough adventurers returned to civilization with gold pieces such as these that the search for El Dorado continued.

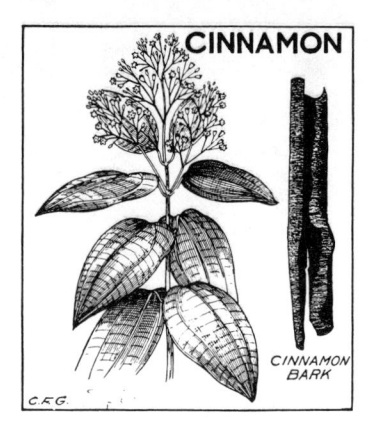

Spices were very highly prized in Europe. Francisco Pizarro and others sought the source of the particularly fine cinnamon they acquired from the Incas.

strength of the El Dorado legend that men continued to explore the interior. Hundreds of expeditions returned to the coastal cities in such dire shape that the hazards of their journeys must have been well known. But enough adventurers returned with golden objects and emeralds that never a month went by that one group or another was not leaving to try its luck, or at least making plans to do so. Once in the interior they felt that if they could just hang on a little longer, get over the next mountain, across an insect-infested swamp, or around the next bend in the river—who knew what wonders might lie ahead?

Gonzalo Pizarro and the Land of Cinnamon

Spices were very highly prized in Europe in the days before refrigeration: They helped preserve food and hid the taste of rotting meat. Vast profits had been made by travelers who brought spices overland from India. It was one of the treasures Columbus had hoped to find—and it was still a way to make a fortune.

When the Spaniards conquered Peru they noticed that the Incas used a form of cinnamon that they obtained from forest tribes east of Quito. Naturally Francisco Pizarro was eager to discover the source of this cinnamon. He urged Gonzalo Diáz de Pineda, the mayor of Quito after Belalcázar, to search for this spice. Pineda did, but the Indians fought him off. He returned with no cinnamon.

But Pineda had learned that farther on there was a broad, flat land full of Indians who all wore gold ornaments. One more mention of gold was all it took to send Gonzalo Pizarro, brother of Francisco, on his way.

Would he find a golden land—and cinnamon too?

In February of 1541, Gonzalo Pizarro and 220 Spaniards under his command marched out of

Quito. Pizarro wrote, "Each man carried only a sword and a shield, with a small sack of food beneath it." Llamas and four thousand Indian porters carried all the heavy loads.

In the wooded hills east of Quito the expedition found none of the convenient Inca roads they thought would be there. They crossed high mountains where many Indians died of cold, and then plunged down into jungles, cutting a path for the horses with axes and machetes. They built bridges to cross rivers, and eventually they did find some cinnamon trees! But the trees were scattered among dense, hilly forests. How could they profitably gather the bark and transport it out of the jungle?

Angry at his lack of success, Pizarro became desperate to find an exit from the jungle. It was the wet season. The forest was dripping with rain, and the ground rapidly turned to slimy pink mud. Flash floods carried away supplies. Months went by. Of all the servants brought from Quito, none remained. Those who did not die fled into the forest. The only way to transport the equipment

Gonzalo Pizarro's expedition travelled with llamas and thousands of Indian porters.

> "The imagination is never satisfied with realities, and El Dorado became a myth and a dream."
>
> Warwick Bray, *The Gold of El Dorado*

> "History is not a science. It is an art. And one succeeds in it mostly by imagination."
>
> Victor W. von Hagen, *The Golden Man*

would be by boat. So a boat was built right there with wood from the surrounding forest.

"Nails were made by converting the iron of the horseshoes of the dead horses into spikes, chicle sap extracted from trees when boiled down became their pitch, and the tattered clothes of those who looked for 'the land of cinnamon' became the oakum for caulking," writes von Hagen. The boat completed, the expedition labored downstream for forty-three days, carrying sick men and equipment such as crossbows, ammunition, and auquebuses (heavy guns fired from a support). Some men, however, struggled along the banks with the horses. The army made little progress. Finally the group divided.

Francisco de Orellana, the second-in-command, took the boat with sixty men aboard to try to find food in a prosperous land the natives said was further downstream to the east. Pizarro waited, encamped on the bank of the river.

Francisco de Orellana's Fascinating Discoveries

The river led forward enticingly, and "Although we wanted to return to the expedition where the Governor [Pizarro] remained behind," wrote Orellana, "it was impossible to go back because of the fact that the currents were too strong." After some weeks, Pizarro made his way back to Quito, but three-quarters of his original force had died of starvation or disease.

Orellana and his men were fairly sure that the rivers to the east of the Andes mountains flowed into the Atlantic Ocean. They probably had no idea that the river they were traveling led to another so wide and powerful. Along the way they found many large settlements, some in which the natives were friendly, some in which they turned hostile when the famished Spaniards ran amok eating the food of the villagers. Many fine roads led away from the settlements, and this

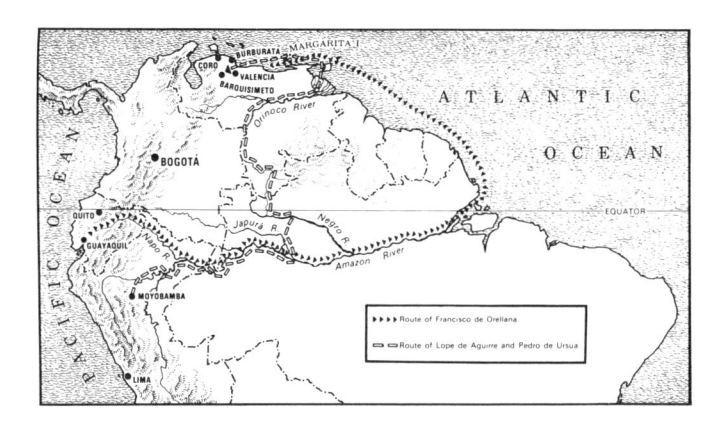

Francisco de Orellana's expedition found many unusual treasures and adventures but no gold.

discovery caused much excitement among the explorers. Did one of these roads lead to El Dorado? Orellana followed some of these, but found they led no farther than plantations behind the villages where maize, manioc (a starchy root plant), yams, beans, peanuts, and gourds were raised.

In the rich villages of the Omagua tribe the explorers were impressed by the fine glazed pottery of these Indians. There were huge jars capable of holding a hundred gallons of liquid. There were plates, bowls, and objects like candelabra, all superbly decorated. The visitors saw some gold objects in the Omagua huts, but were afraid to take them as they wanted to escape alive.

They also saw something very strange. The Indians had a custom of flattening their children's heads so they bulged sideways like hammerhead sharks! In a land of such peculiarities, what else might be found?

Weeks on the Amazon

The men in the expedition became eager to explore farther. They built a second, larger and stronger, boat to supplement the first. They entered the main branch of the river now known as the Amazon in mid-February 1542, and cruised down its swirling waters for weeks on end.

Author John Hemming writes:

> The Amazon near the Omagua lands is as broad as a lake, and its mass of gently flowing water is the colour of an Indian's skin. The banks are unbroken walls of dark green vegetation, with the great trees masked by a screen of undergrowth.... Immense formations of clouds pile up or race across the heavens, soaking up the moisture of the Amazon forests or turning purple-black with tropical storms. At dawn and sunset the surface of the river mirrors a dazzling spectacle of colour, from silver to golden orange or violet.... Day after day, there is only the immensely broad, placid river and the unbroken lines of trees.

The explorers must have found the region wonderfully mysterious. They honored their leader by naming the river after him.

However, the name was soon changed to its present one because of what happened after the group passed the place where the Madeira River enters from the south. Here they were beset by masses of warriors. Five Spaniards were struck before ever reaching the shore. The chronicler of the expedition, Dominican friar Gaspar de Carvajal, was hit by an arrow that pierced his rib cage.

The Amazon River was wide, long, and bordered by thick jungle.

He wrote, "Had it not been for the thickness of my habit [the friar's garment], that would have been the end of me." The fierce fight lasted scarcely an hour before the Spaniards escaped in their boats, drifting off with the current, too exhausted to row.

They did, however, manage to capture one Indian. He told them that these warriors were so determined to defend their land because they were the subjects of a tribe of warlike women.

Carvajal wrote:

> We ourselves saw ten or twelve of these women, fighting there in front of all the Indian men as female captains. They fought so courageously that the men did not dare turn their backs. They killed any [Indian men] who did turn back, with their clubs, right there in front of us, which is why the Indians kept up their defences for so long. These women are very white and tall, with very long braided hair wound about their heads. They are very robust, and go naked with their private parts covered, with bows and arrows in

The Spanish explorers often faced hostile Indian tribes.

The conquistadores heard tales of a formidable tribe of women warriors.

their hands, doing as much fighting as ten Indian men.... And indeed there was one woman among these who shot an arrow a span [about nine inches] into one of the brigantines [boats]; others did the same until our brigantines looked like porcupines.

The captured Indian also told Carvajal that he had often visited the villages of these women, a week's march to the north of the river. What he said reminded Orellana of the Greek legend of the Amazons, a race of warrior women who did not permit men to live among them. Carvajal thereafter referred to these Indian women as Amazons, and renamed the river after them.

The Land of Warrior Women

The Spaniards were evidently fascinated with what the captive Indian said, for Carvajal extracted more information about this fierce tribe from him:

The Indian said that their [the women warriors] houses were of stone and with regular doors, and that from one village to another went roads... with guards stationed at intervals along them so that no one might enter without paying duty. The

Captain asked if these women bore children; the Indian answered that they did. He asked him how, not being married, and there being no man residing among them, they became pregnant; he replied that these Indian women consorted with Indian men at times, when desire came over them. They also assembled a great horde of warriors and went off to make war on a very great chieftain whose residence is not far from the land of these women, and so by force they brought them to their own country and kept them with them for the time that suited their caprice, and after they found themselves pregnant they sent them back to their country without doing them any harm. Afterwards, when the time came for them to have children, if they gave birth to male children they killed them or sent them to their fathers, and if females, they raised them with great care and instructed them in the arts of war.

He said that there was in their possession a very great wealth of gold and silver, and that in the case of all women of rank and distinction their eating utensils were nothing but gold or silver, while the other women, belonging to the plebeian class, used a service of wooden vessels and clay. He said that in the capital and principal city in which the ruling mistress resided, there were five very large buildings, which were places of worship, and houses dedicated to the Sun... and that inside, from half of a man's height above the ground up, these buildings were lined with heavy wooden ceilings covered with paint of various colours, and that in these buildings they had many gold and silver idols in the form of women, and many vessels of gold and silver for the service of the Sun.

Stories of Amazon women have fascinated people for years. But did this tribe ever really exist? Do they still?

It is hard to argue with an eyewitness account. Gaspar de Carvajal wrote, "We ourselves saw ten or twelve of these women."

"Chance had brought a myth [of the Amazons] into reality."

Caspar Montibelli, *The World's Last Mysteries*

"The kingdom of women, the Amazons, was [an] illusion."

Victor W. von Hagen, *The Golden Man*

But another historian, Francisco López de Gómara, angrily recalled that other explorers had heard tales of Amazons in the Americas, and he did not believe them. He wrote, "No such thing has ever been seen along this river, and never will be seen!"

Author Victor W. von Hagen, too, questions the credibility of what Carvajal reported. He calls the Amazons a myth, growing out of "a confused knowledge of the Inca 'Chosen Women' of Peru." These were women who served in the Sun Temples. They were enclosed in a kind of convent from which men were excluded. These Sun Maidens were real. But what about the Amazons?

John Hemming calls the Amazons "an elusive tribe of sexually-liberated women," but does not indicate whether he believes they ever did—or still do—exist.

Apparently no one knows for sure. But there are to this day vast areas of the rain forests that remain hidden from exploration.

What did Orellana accomplish? H. J. Mozans, author of *The Quest of El Dorado*, writes, "Outside of the discovery of the Amazon [river] by Orellana, which was incidental, [the net result of the expedition] was virtually *nil*. . . . Beyond certain vague rumors of a rich and powerful chief living somewhere between the Amazon and the Rio Negro they could secure no information regarding the Gilded King and the province of gold that were the objects of their quest."

After encountering the warrior women, Orellana sailed his boat, the *San Pedro*, out of the mouth of the Amazon River and on to Santo Domingo. From there he sailed to Spain where he reported his discovery of the Amazons. Once more people in Europe had something new to marvel at, and it was not difficult for Orellana to raise funds to mount another expedition. He was

Eyewitness accounts from the time of the Spanish explorers confirm the existence of the Amazons. But many modern historians do not believe these accounts are reliable sources of information.

The South American rainforest was a challenge to the Europeans.

given the title of "Governor of the Amazons." With five hundred men, he set out again for the New World to search for El Dorado.

He never found it. Francisco de Orellana died on the return trip, on shipboard, within sight of the Amazon River which he had named.

Where Next?

Within a few years of Orellana's discovery, other conquistadores hunting for El Dorado traversed the jungles of the upper Amazon valley. Heat, exhaustion, disease, starvation, and hostile Indians destroyed one expedition after another. No one got any closer to the elusive kingdom of the Golden Man. John Hemming says, "the supposed location of El Dorado and his kingdom withdrew farther and farther into the remaining, unexplored portion of the interior. Finally, there was nowhere left for it to be found except in the dim fastnesses [remote and secluded areas] of 'Guiana,' the name by which the Spaniards knew the great unmapped basin of the Orinoco [River] and its tributaries."

The lure of El Dorado was like a magnet pulling men into the unknown. Perhaps none felt this pull more deeply than a leader who made the search his personal goal.

Antonio de Berrio

According to author Timothy Severin, Antonio de Berrio came to the search for El Dorado by accident. He was a professional soldier who had served a full and very active life in the armies of Emperor Charles V and had reached the rank of captain. He was an outstanding officer.

Then his wife's uncle died, leaving Berrio his estate. This somewhat distant relative was none other than Jiménez de Quesada! Berrio had heard rumors that Quesada had made a huge fortune for himself during his conquest of the Chibcha Indians in Colombia. Severin says Berrio might have seen his legacy as an ideal opportunity to retire and enjoy the sand and sea breezes of the golden land, not to mention the yearly income of fourteen thousand ducats which the property in the New World was said to be worth. Berrio loaded his family and belongings aboard a convoy and sailed to the islands of the Antilles in 1580.

If retirement was what Berrio had planned, he must have changed his mind. Quesada's will contained a clause saying that the heir to his estate must use part of the income to finance the search for El Dorado. Berrio had plenty of money and could have hired someone to conduct the search. Instead, he climbed back in the saddle and began leading troops on long treks into the interior. Perhaps he is one of the people Alvin Schwartz is

This map from the fifteenth century shows the unusually broad mouth of the Orinoco River. Many explorers thought that somewhere near the banks of the Orinoco was the ceremonial lake the Indians threw their golden treasures into.

referring to in his book, *Gold & Silver, Silver & Gold*, when he says, "Everyone who hunts for treasure dreams of striking it rich. But often it is more than money that attracts them. It is the hunt itself."

Whatever his motivation, Berrio was eager to explore. He heard that somewhere on the right bank of the Orinoco River was a huge lake where a great and powerful tribe lived in splendor. Berrio tried to find this lake. He traveled down the length of the Orinoco, attempting to lead exploring parties up its right-bank tributaries. But, says Severin,

> On every occasion his progress was blocked by a range of mountains which ran parallel with the Orinoco. He surmised that these might be the

Berrio thought the mountains which ran alongside the Orinoco might be those rumored to surround the lake of the El Dorado legend.

The route followed by Berrio in quest of El Dorado.

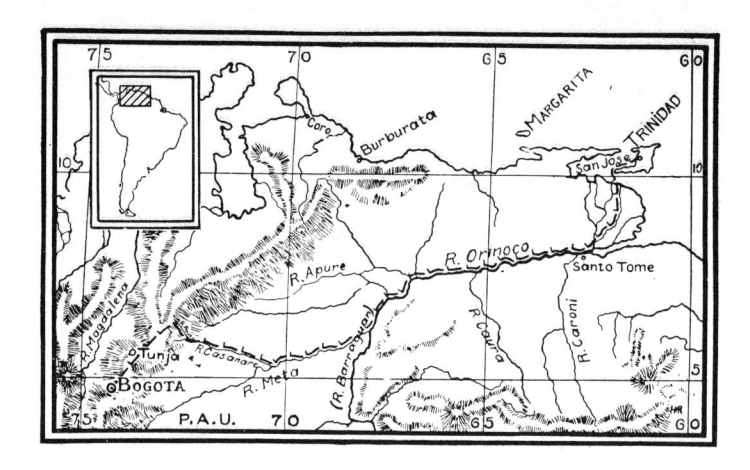

mountains which were supposed to surround the lake of the El Dorado legend, and he was heartened to hear from the natives that the powerful tribe on the lake had arrived only some twenty years earlier, and had established their supremacy with payments of gold and irresistible military organization.

Certainly this tribe was the fugitive group from Peru which had fled from Pizarro's army! The gold they carried was the treasure they had salvaged from the Incas!

Berrio made three journeys to find this treasure. They spanned thirteen years, including preparation time between each trip. V. S. Naipaul, in *The Loss of El Dorado*, says that for Berrio, "the search had become a way of life." At one point a chief called Moriquito told Berrio it was only a four-day march to El Dorado, but Berrio quarreled with Moriquito and decided to move on in another direction.

Berrio did not find El Dorado. But his interest continued, especially when a man named Albujar said he had visited the city of the Gilded Man!

Juan Martinez de Albujar's Story

Juan Martinez de Albujar was the sole survivor of a lost expedition to El Dorado that had vanished ten years earlier. After stumbling out of the interior, he dramatically appeared in the church in Margarita near the mouth of the Amazon River. He asked for confession.

Albujar was dressed in the clothes of an Indian chief and he spoke broken Spanish, as though, says Severin, "the words were strange to him." For years, Albujar claimed, he had been living among the tribes of the interior and they had taken him to visit the city of the Gilded Man. He had been led blindfolded through the jungle for many days, and when the blindfold was removed from his eyes he had found himself standing at the outskirts of a city so vast that it had taken him and his guides from dawn to dusk to walk from the main gate to the palace of the ruler. In the great palace he had seen "with his own eyes" the Gilded Man and his courtiers glistening in their golden skins. For seven months he had witnessed the grandeur of El Dorado, and the Gilded Man himself had welcomed him and questioned him about the ways of white men. Then Albujar had been released. His eyes were covered once more, and he was escorted back through the jungle.

As a farewell gift the Gilded Man had given him a quantity of gold and jewels, which, Albujar said, had been stolen from him by forest Indians as he made his way back to the Spanish settlements. All he had left were a few gold beads. To prove his story, he showed this evidence and offered to swear on the Bible that he was telling the truth.

Some people thought Albujar's long stay in the jungle had unhinged his mind. V. S. Naipaul even says, "Albujar may never have existed. No one [but the priest] saw him, and...no one saw the gold beads; they were left with Albujar's confessor to pay for masses [in the church]." Then

One tale says that Juan Martinez de Albujar actually saw the Golden Man and his kingdom. There was no reliable evidence to confirm his story, however.

> "The notable fact is that there once was a Golden Man and there was a lake in which he made his golden ablutions. It is as true a history as one can forge."
>
> Victor W. von Hagen, *The Golden Man*

> "They never found the golden city, for it existed only in their dreams."
>
> Alvin Schwartz, *Gold & Silver, Silver & Gold*

was the priest-confessor who related the story lying?

Some authors who wrote about Albujar say he was positively identified by men who had known him before he had left the settlement to hunt for El Dorado. They said he had a plausible answer to every skeptical question. Eventually, say those who believe Albujar was real, it was decided there was enough truth in what he said that he should go to Spain to tell of his adventure there. Presumably that would create more interest so Europeans would finance further expeditions. But Albujar never reached his country. When his ship stopped in Puerto Rico he caught a fever and died, still clinging to his story, even on his deathbed.

If Albujar was a real person, did he actually visit the fabulous realm of El Dorado? If he did not, why did so many people—including Antonio de Berrio—believe in him and his story?

Berrio Makes Plans

Berrio was re-inspired by the story of Albujar and he planned a fourth journey. Every detail that Albujar recited seemed to confirm what Berrio had already learned about the upper reaches of the Orinoco. In addition, he was certain he now knew the name of the lake on which El Dorado was found. It was Lake Manoa, and it was so large that it took the Indians three days to paddle their canoes across it! Even though Berrio was now seventy years old, his adventuring spirit could not be stilled.

As it turned out, he never made his fourth journey. He made long preparations for it, and in the midst of these he directed a Spaniard named Domingo de Vera to take possession of the lands along the Orinoco. This Vera did, returning with seventeen golden eagles and jackals, finely worked. According to V. S. Naipaul:

He [Domingo de Vera] brought more than gold: he said he had found El Dorado. He spoke of the cold, high city with its temples full of gold. He spoke of a clothed, civilized, artistic people who had...come from the west; just twenty years before they had conquered the jungle Indians.

It was the old story, but it was what the Spaniards wanted to hear. In the retelling, the seventeen eagles and jackals became forty of the most pure plates of gold, swords inlaid with gold, and a golden idol. Eventually those seventeen items turned into two million objects of gold!

Antonio de Berrio wrote to King Philip II announcing the discovery of El Dorado. The Indians had told Vera that a thousand men would be needed to capture El Dorado. Such a force was beyond Berrio's resources and he needed help from the king.

Before it could arrive, four vessels appeared off the island of Trinidad. As the Spanish watched, the crews of the strange vessels prepared a flotilla of launches, provisioning them for what was clearly a trip up the Orinoco River—Berrio's territory. He immediately dispatched a squad of heavily armed soldiers to the beach to demand the identity of the interlopers.

To his dismay, Berrio learned that the ships were English. Their commander's name was Sir Walter Raleigh, and he had arrived to search for El Dorado.

The Quest of Sir Walter Raleigh

When Sir Walter Raleigh left England in 1595 to risk his fortune and his life in the Caribbean sun, he had already made a name for himself at home. He had been a soldier and a captain of the Queen's Guard. He had been made a knight and acquired a small private fortune. But because he had married Queen Elizabeth's maid, Raleigh fell into disfavor with the ruling monarch. In an ef-

King Philip II. Antonio de Berrio requested the king's help in providing the necessary resources to continue the search for El Dorado.

Sir Walter Raleigh, knight, adventurer, and the first Englishman to enter into the search for El Dorado.

fort to regain favor at court, he hit upon the idea of finding the Golden Man before the Spanish did. Surely this discovery would bring him additional wealth, please the queen, and thrust him back into the limelight that he craved.

According to author Timothy Severin, Raleigh "went about the matter thoroughly." He ferreted out everything that was known about the Gilded Man, questioning captains of vessels and travelers who had visited the Spanish colonies in the Americas. He ransacked the libraries for information.

"The truth of the matter was," says Severin, "that Raleigh...was aiming at no less than a complete English empire in South America, and already he had a name for it—'Guiana,' the word which Juan Martinez de Albujar had used in connection with the realm of the Gilded Man."

The final bits of information about El Dorado came his way in 1594, when an English privateer (a private ship commissioned to attack enemy warships) under the command of Captain George Popham intercepted a Spanish ship. The ship was boarded and looted and all her documents seized. Among them was a bundle of letters which carefully spelled out all evidence supporting the El Dorado theory.

The same year news arrived in England that Antonio de Berrio had ambushed and massacred eight English sailors who had gone ashore at Trinidad hunting for fresh meat. Severin explains that instead of frightening Raleigh off, this incident led him to think that Berrio believed very seriously in an El Dorado on the Orinoco and was protecting the mouth of the river from foreign invaders. It was time for the English to intervene before it was too late.

A Deadly Goal

Raleigh's expedition was hastily thrown

Sir Walter Raleigh wanted to win glory at the English court. In pursuit of that, he captured Spanish explorer Antonio de Berrio and murdered his men. This eliminated an important rival to the fame and fortune Raleigh sought in the New World.

together. The English government somewhat grudgingly gave him an official commission, instructing him to "offend and enfeeble the King of Spain."

Raleigh was delighted when his ships at last reached Trinidad. He took notes on the outline of the coast, the soil, and the plants and animals. Besides hoping to find gold, Raleigh was eager to record the "curiosities" to be seen and to observe the "naturals," as he called the natives. He experimented with new materials such as some pitch he found in a lake and used to caulk his ship. His energy and enthusiasm were formidable. And he was deadly serious.

When he encountered Berrio and his men, Raleigh sent a boatload of food and drink to the Spaniards guarding the landing place. When these men had settled down to their supper, Raleigh's men surrounded and massacred them.

Most of the Spanish garrison was killed and Berrio was taken prisoner. The English soldiers then went through the settlement looking for papers and valuables, and in the end set the village

A fanciful painting of Sir Walter Raleigh exploring the Orinoco River and confronting its dangers.

of St. Joseph on fire. Raleigh tried to pump Berrio for information, but to no avail. In spite of threats to his life, Berrio only told of the discomforts and dangers of the interior.

Taking Berrio along as hostage, Raleigh and his flotilla made a shaky start up the Orinoco River. They promptly lost their way. They found the delta of this river to be immense, a huge maze of streams and rivers that looped, divided, and rejoined in bewildering confusion. Additionally, thick, unfriendly green forest came down to the very edge of the swirling muddy waters.

Raleigh wrote, "We might have wandered a whole year in that labyrinth of rivers," but good luck saved them from disaster. They surprised a party of three Indians in a canoe and made friendly gestures. With the Indians' help, they were able to make their way into the main channel.

A cacique called Topiawari gave Raleigh a garbled tribal history that included tales of the Incas who "came from so far off as the sun slept."

He also told of the mountains of Guiana and the city of gold. Yet, as always, the cacique did not know the route which led across the mountains to this fabulous land. His best advice was to continue upstream until they reached the mouth of the Caroni, a large tributary which veered to the right of the Orinoco. The Caroni, suggested Topiawari, was the key to El Dorado. This was precisely the kind of vague half-promise that had misled the Spanish conquistadores for nearly seventy years.

Monotony Sets In

But oddly enough, instead of rushing off after his dream, Raleigh seemed to have lost his enthusiasm. He went off on a series of side trips which gained him nothing. When he finally headed toward the Caroni, he went no further than the mouth of this river! His only excuse, which he later made to his backers in England, was that the rising flood waters in the Orinoco made it impossible for the expedition to continue. He was also worried about his men left waiting

The native chief Topiawari brought Raleigh gifts and advice.

A sixteenth-century drawing of Indians panning for gold.

for him at Point Icacos, at the mouth of the Orinoco.

Severin says neither explanation "carried much weight. He could just as easily have spent a few more days or even weeks, before the floods became too dangerous, or he could have transferred the expedition from the boats and struck overland toward the mountains. And as for the fleet at Icacos, there was no reason for him to be so suddenly concerned about its safety."

More likely, Raleigh felt that this uncomfortable journey into the wilds had gone on too long. He had grown bored. Every bend of the river looked monotonously like the last. Perhaps too, his men had tired of the temperature and the humidity that made their clothes rot on their backs. Perhaps they remembered the fate of the young man who had rashly gone for a swim in the river—and had been attacked by a crocodile. He had been dragged under and drowned in full view of his companions.

Return to Civilization

Whatever the reasons, Raleigh decided to return to Trinidad. He did, however, take the trouble to first walk over to see the waterfalls where the Caroni River met the Orinoco. Here, with daggers and their hands, some of the English sailors dug out any rock or pebble which looked as if it might contain traces of gold. Raleigh warned them that they were wasting their time. He believed that gold-bearing rock would lie several feet underground. Falling back to Topiawari's village, the party made plans to return to England.

The return trip down the Orinoco was no picnic either. The water level had begun to rise, and the current was treacherous. Two or three times a day torrential downpours cascaded from the sky, blotting out the shore. From time to time the men stopped to get supplies from the natives. Raleigh took these opportunities to visit the Cacaque people and tell them of his plan to oust the Spaniards from their lands.

One Indian chief by the name of Putijma intercepted the Englishmen while they were going downstream. He told them of a mountain which he claimed "had stones of the cullor of golde." This was too tempting to pass up, but after a half-day's journey on shore, Raleigh turned back with his main party. He sent Keymis, his chief lieutenant, to press ahead with a squad of six men.

Keymis went only so far as he had to to see the so-called golden mountain. When he rejoined the flotilla, Keymis reported that there was a potential gold mine near Putijma's village. Raleigh took his word for it. Checking it out further would have to wait until a time when Raleigh could return with a larger and better-equipped force. The party continued downstream.

Apparently Raleigh had grown fond of his prisoner, Governor Berrio, for, as the ships headed for England by way of Venezuela, he set Berrio free.

Raleigh's expedition had been gone seven

"The Ewaipanoma, Raleigh wrote, were a freakish tribe of club-wielding giants.... He had never actually seen any of them, but the Orinoco Indians had solemnly assured him that such a tribe really existed."

Timothy Severin, *The Golden Antilles*

"The lunacy of the Golden Man must have destroyed all of the deductive reasoning of Sir Walter."

Victor W. von Hagen, *The Golden Man*

Raleigh's route. He turned back long before finding the fabled city of gold.

months. During that time he and a small squadron of Englishmen had penetrated three hundred miles up the Orinoco River, farther than any English had gone before. But that was the limit of his achievement. His attempt to find the kingdom of the Gilded Man and to start a rich new colony had failed. Raleigh brought back nothing more than a handful of Indian trinkets, some tobacco looted from St. Joseph, a few pieces of what might or might not be gold ore, and several more rumors to add to the lore of the Gilded Man and his whereabouts.

A Lukewarm Welcome

Raleigh's reception back in England was lukewarm. His investors were disgruntled at having made no profit on the venture, and his enemies laughed. Some of them claimed Raleigh had never left England at all. They said he had been hiding in comfort in remote bays off the English coast. Others said he had gone as far as Africa and the little gold he brought back was picked up there. To make matters worse, the "gold ore" that had been scratched out at Caroni Falls against Raleigh's advice proved to have no trace of gold at all.

Raleigh had to defend himself. He did so with his pen. He published a personal account of the Guiana trip called *The Discovery*. It was beautifully written, but he could not resist including some extraordinary stories of this new land. One of the most outlandish was about the Ewaipanoma Indian tribe. Author Severin says:

> The Ewaipanoma, Raleigh wrote, were a freakish tribe of club-wielding giants who lived in the remote fastnesses (isolation) of Guiana. He himself had never actually seen any of them, but the Orinoco Indians had solemnly assured him that such a tribe really existed, and they even claimed that they had captured an Ewaipanoma in battle. According to the Indians, these giants were true monstrosities, for they had no heads. And since they were headless, their eyes, nose, and mouths were...located in the middle of their chests, while a thatch of long hair grew backward from their shoulders.

This preposterous yarn, as Raleigh should have known, was one of the oldest of all travelers' tales. Its origins went back more than a thousand years, and during the Middle Ages the same headless giants had appeared in the *Travels* of author Sir John Mandeville. By the sixteenth century, in fact, the fable of the "men with their eyes beneath their shoulders" was beginning to be recognized as humbug. So it was all the more remarkable that Raleigh chose to dust off the myth and parade it forth once again as though it were true. He explained that since many of Mandeville's tall stories had turned out to be based on fact, there

The title page of Raleigh's book about his travels in America. Although it held sound information, it also contained far-fetched tales.

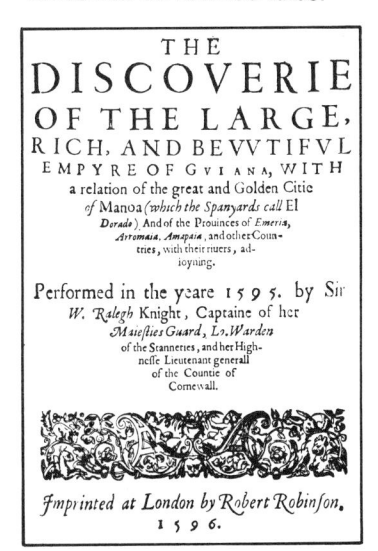

was no reason to suppose that a tribe of headless men did not exist in the depths of the Guiana jungle.

Severin suggests that

> More cynically, perhaps, Raleigh had resurrected the monstrous Ewaipanoma because he knew that the taller his story, the more it would delight his...readers and draw attention to his book. In fact the tale became one of *The Discovery's* most popular, and in some cases most ridiculed, passages, with later editions showing fanciful pictures of the hideous Ewaipanoma with great war clubs in their hands and surly scowls on their chests. In the long run, however, the story of the headless men probably did more harm than good, for it reduced the overall credibility of *The Discovery*....The headless men were sufficiently notorious to make other stories in the book less believable.

Spreading Fantasies in the Old World

Although Raleigh's book was a popular success, it did not impress the queen, nor the people who could finance a further trip for his dream of colonization. It did, however, enchant other dreamers, for somehow Raleigh seemed to forget

Among other "wonders" described in Raleigh's book was a tribe of headless natives!

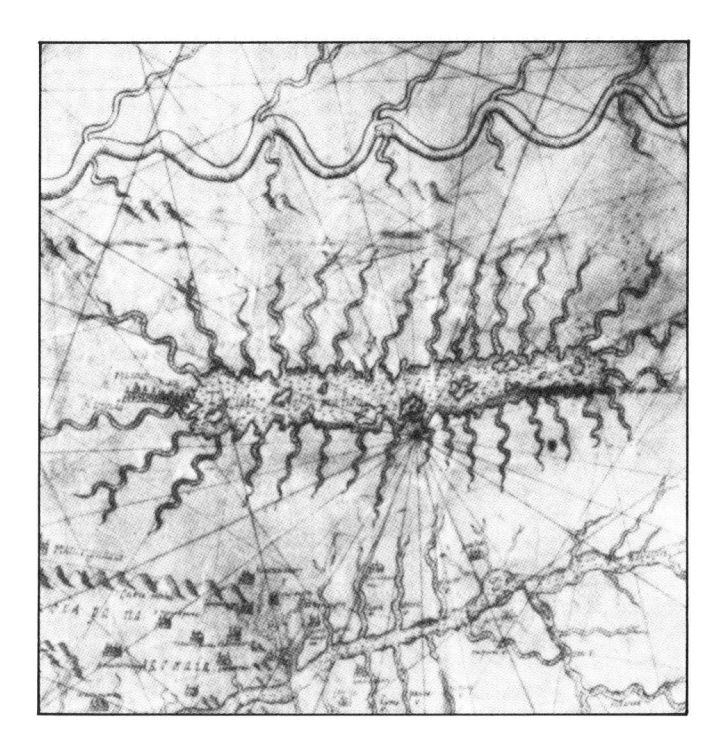

This map was drawn at Raleigh's instruction. Lake Manoa is the "centipede" at the center of the map, between the Amazon River on the north and the Orinoco on the south. Raleigh and others thought Lake Manoa had golden cities along its shores. Despite the distortions in this map, for many years it remained one of the best sources of knowledge about the geography of South America.

what his journey on the Orinoco had really been like. In *The Discovery*, he wrote that the countryside was:

> All faire greene grasse, the ground of hard sand easy to march on, eyther for horse or foote, the deere crossing in every path, the birds towardes the evening singing on every tree with a thousand several tunes, cranes and herons of white, crimson, and carnation perching on the rivers side, the ayre fresh with a gentle easterlie wind, and every stone that we stooped to take up, promised eyther gold or silver by his complexion.

Editions of this travelogue were printed in Germany and the Netherlands, doing their share toward spreading the truths, half-truths, and fantasies of the New World.

About the same time that the book was published, Raleigh made a notable contribution to geographical knowledge. His "Guiana map"

Sir Walter Raleigh's life ended in disgrace.

showed a large segment of South America lying between the mouth of the Amazon and the Isthmus of Panama. Von Hagen says it was "as precise and correct as any map of the time," with one glaring inaccuracy. Behind the clearly marked line of the "mountains of Guiana" was the tantalizing outline of a huge lake. This was placed between the Amazon and Orinoco rivers and resembled a giant centipede. It was, so it was said, the Lake of Manoa—seven hundred miles long and fed by hundreds of streams. Raleigh claimed that on its shores were the great and golden cities, including the one the Spaniards called El Dorado. This lake, also known as Parima, remained on maps for the next 150 years.

Raleigh must have convinced himself, if very few others, that the golden land still beckoned. The hope of finding it sustained him during the thirteen months he spent in the Tower of London, accused of treason.

During his stay in the tower, Raleigh never

abandoned his dream. He sent a trading vessel to the Orinoco delta every second year at his own expense with orders to maintain contact with the "naturals." Reports from the New World indicated that the Spaniards had fortified their position along the Caroni River. Captain Keymis believed they had done so because they had opened gold mines there. The Spaniards were, in fact, expecting to uncover the gold they suspected had lured Raleigh to Guiana. Thus, each side convinced the other that a fortune would be found in the Orinoco basin.

Raleigh repeatedly petitioned King James to free him and send him on an expedition. Finally, because the king was desperately short of money, he agreed. He hoped Raleigh would find gold to solve his financial problems.

This time Raleigh's efforts were directed toward finding mines, not El Dorado or the Golden City. He put together an impressive-looking fleet, but things went wrong from the start. The weather caused numerous delays. And once the fleet was underway, illness claimed many sailors' lives. Raleigh himself became seriously ill. Things were little better when they reached land. Severin calls Raleigh's second expedition a "catastrophe." But, Severin adds, "The Orinoco mines, Raleigh stubbornly maintained, really existed."

Raleigh's life ended in disgrace. He was again accused of treason, and he was beheaded on October 29, 1618.

Still, author John Hemming says, "It was Walter Raleigh who popularized the legend of El Dorado."

Five

A Mixture of Fantasy and Reality?

By the end of the sixteenth century the lure of El Dorado had taken conquistadores from the Andean highlands of what is now Peru, Ecuador, and Colombia, to the forests of Venezuela and Brazil. Each expedition had lasted from two to five years. "The road to Eldorado was littered with corpses of captains, soldiers, and Indians," writes Caspar Montibelli in *The Search for Eldorado*. "Except for a few nuggets of gold, a sizeable haul of emeralds and some cinnamon, there was little to show for nearly a century of exploration. No one had found the Golden Man or discovered his treasure."

But the treasure of El Dorado cannot be dismissed so easily. The "few nuggets of gold" that Caspar Montibelli mentions were in reality tons of gold, much of it melted down by the Spaniards and sent back to Europe as gold and silver bars. And there is evidence that ceremonies in which precious articles were thrown into lakes really did take place. Some of the most solid evidence was brought to light by a rich merchant of Bogotá even before the sixteenth century ended.

Draining Lake Guatavita

In 1580, Antonio Sepúlveda secured permis-

An early illustration showing the Spanish on the never-ending search for gold.

> "The lake on which these offerings of gold and emeralds was made, was Guatavita, a short distance to the northeast of Bogota."
>
> Sixteenth-century chronicler Juan Rodriguez Freyle

> "The Muisca, with no gold mines of their own, would never have thrown much treasure into these waters."
>
> Adventurer Col. J. P. Hamilton, at a visit to Lake Guatavita in 1826

sion from Spain to search Lake Guatavita for its treasure. In return, he was to give to the crown one-fifth of all he found.

Author Victor W. von Hagen explains that some golden offerings called *tunjos*, which are of base copper with only a slight golden skin, had previously been uncovered around the edges of the lake bed during the dry seasons. "Pure gold, having three times the specific gravity of iron, would, with the passage of time, have slipped down the mud banks into the deeper part of the funnel-shaped lake." So Sepúlveda had strong reason to believe the lake bed would hold untold treasure. He prepared to drain Lake Guatavita.

Sepúlveda knew it would be no easy task. He began operations by building houses along the lakeshore for the workers who would be helping him in his search. He took soundings of the lake from a boat. He assembled Indian laborers—approximately eight thousand—and set them to work cutting a great notch in the rim of the lake. Von Hagen says the Indians "worked like harvester ants." The earth they pried out was put in their poncho-like *ruanas* and carried away. In time, months at least, a large V-shaped slice was cut into the lake crater.

Water poured out! Unhappily, it gushed out with such force it took with it a number of Indians. But at the edge of the lake, buried in the mud, were golden images and an emerald as large as an egg. Historian Pedro Simon describes more of Sepúlveda's finds: There were "breastplates or pectoral discs, serpents, eagles, a staff covered with gold plaques and hung with little golden tubes...making a total of five or six ducats for the royal treasury."

The original records have now been found, and according to Hemming, 232 pesos and ten grams of good gold were all Sepúlveda found. But

Antonio Sepúlveda was the first to attempt to drain Lake Guatavita to find its gold.

the amount is not as important as the fact that he had proved there was gold in the depths of Lake Guatavita.

Juan Rodriguez Freyle, one of Sepúlveda's friends, wrote that "much later, the desire came over him [Sepúlveda] to make another attempt at drainage, but he could not, and in the end he died poor and tired."

With such evidence it was natural that others would attempt to finish what Sepúlveda had started. In 1625, twelve people applied for permission to search for gold, silver, pearls, and other things of value in the lake. But "nothing came of this," says Hemming.

Further Attempts

The days of the Spanish conquistadores were over by the time the next attempt to drain the lake was made. Interest in the project flared when Alexander von Humboldt, the foremost naturalist of his day, arrived in South America in 1799 to study the geology, botany, and geography of the area. He spent two months in Bogotá, during which time he visited Lake Guatavita. Although interested primarily in scientific findings, von Humboldt commented on Sepúlveda's cut, which was (and is to this day) still a prominent part of the landscape. Von Humboldt noted on the banks of the lake "the remains of a staircase, hewn in the rock and serving for the ceremonial of ablution [religious cleansing]." This staircase was not mentioned in any other writings by other scholars and added a new bit of mystery to the rituals which had almost certainly taken place there.

Apparently even the scientist von Humboldt could not resist the lure of El Dorado, for author von Hagen says:

> When back in Paris, and coming to that section of his scientific travels, he [Humboldt] computed that if a thousand Indians a year had made their annual pilgrimage thence to Guatavita for a century, as had been claimed, further, if each had thrown a minimum of five golden trinkets into the lake to honor the resident deity, then there were upwards of 50,000,000 golden pieces buried in the thick black ooze at the bottom of the lake. Humboldt's calculation, taking the price of gold then in 1807, was that the gold in Guatavita would have a current monetary value of some $3,000,000,000. When this was read by Monsieur de la Kier of the Royal Institute of Paris, he himself revised Humboldt's estimate of the worth of cash value then of the golden Chibcha objects that lay at the bottom of Lake Guatavita. His estimate: $5,600,000,000.

The value would be much greater today!

Von Humboldt did not pursue the matter, but his calculations inspired "Pepe" Paris, a citizen of Bogotá, to try to empty the lake. His attempts, too, were unsuccessful. Lake Guatavita would not give up its treasure.

If Guatavita could not be drained, treasure hunters thought that perhaps other treasure-laden

Opposite: Alexander von Humboldt camped beside the Orinoco River.

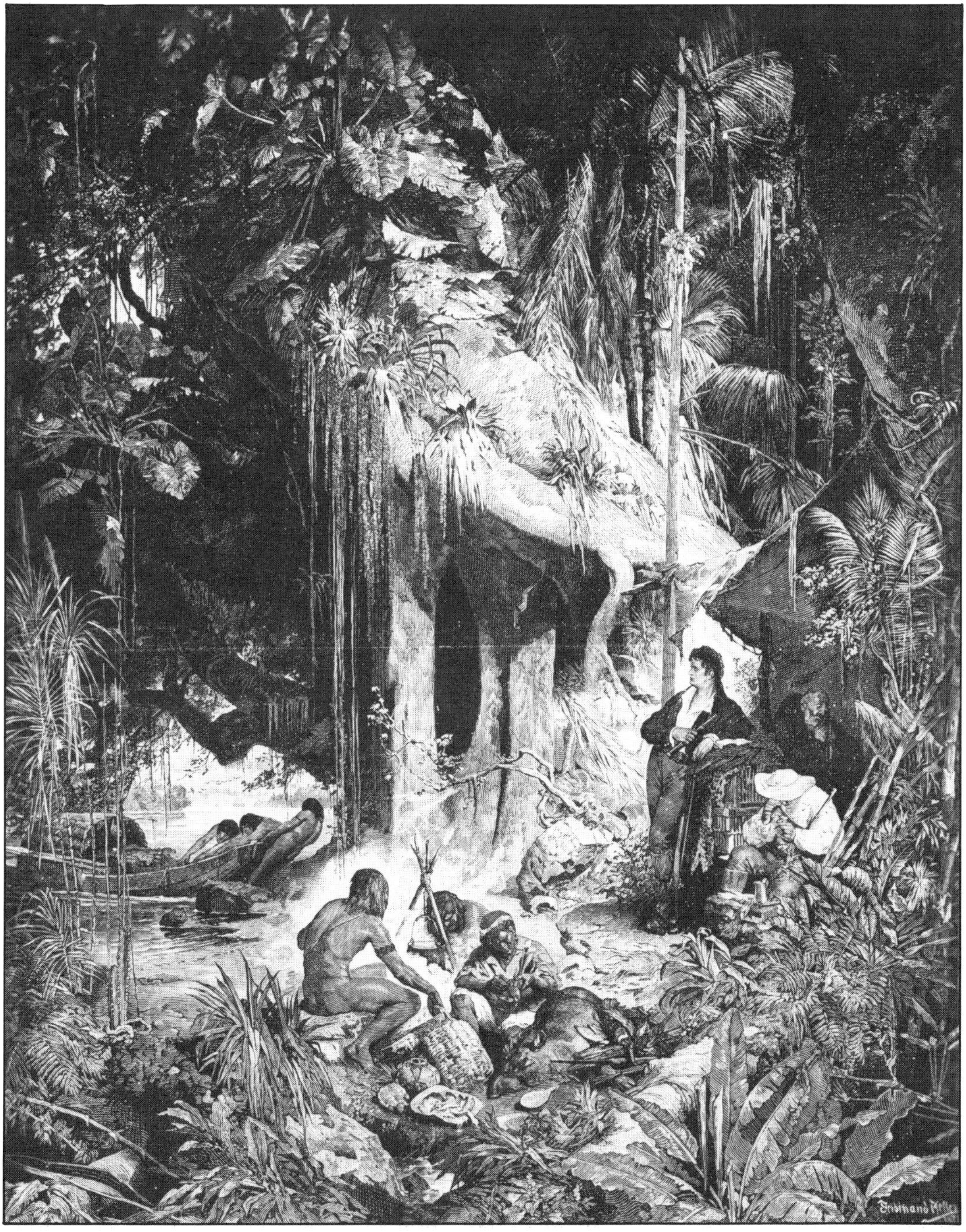

lakes could. They had learned that there were many holy lakes. Besides Guatavita, there were Lake Guasca, Lake Siecha, Lake Teusacá, and Lake Ubaque. All of these were pilgrimage centers where idols were set up and offerings were made. What might be found there?

An Exciting Discovery at Lake Siecha

Siecha is another round lake in an isolated area south of the village of Guatavita. A company that was formed to drain this lake reasoned that there may have been a mistake in the tales of El Dorado. Siecha might have been the lake used for the Chibcha ceremony, not Lake Guatavita. Besides, it might contain treasures thrown into it when the natives tried to escape the conquistadores.

The first attempt to drain the lake failed, but a second attempt, in 1856, resulted in a channel dug three meters deep and fifty meters long. The lake was lowered by a full three meters (over eleven feet). Some Muisca (Chibcha) objects were found, including a golden figure of a chief and ten attendants on a raft. "This extraordinary work seems to confirm the most widespread version of the El Dorado story," writes Henry Wiencek in *The Kings of El Dorado*. "Cast in gold, the eight-inch-long piece is a Muisca tunjo—a votive offering [given in gratitude] placed in sacred grounds and lagoons."

"The raft is only 19.5 centimetres long (about seven and one half inches)," says John Hemming, "but beautifully detailed, with six outer rows of logs curving inwards at the ends and enclosing a central section covered in matting. There are ten attendants on the raft, all flat, triangular figures with features and limbs of wire-thin gold, in typical Muisca style. They wear diadems [crowns] that probably represent feather headdresses. The central figure towers above the rest, although his

In 1856, this ceremonial ornament, a golden raft only about 7½ inches long, was found in Lake Siecha.

height is only 10 centimetres. All the figures face forward. Their careful grouping and static postures leave no doubt that they are performing a ritual."

But Hemming believes it is important to place this raft in perspective. He writes:

> It evidently portrays a ceremony on a lake. But it is only one of thousands of surviving gold Muisca artifacts. Worship of lakes was only one element in Muisca religion. The first observers of Muisca society wrote much about its religion but scarcely mentioned the importance of lakes, for the Muisca worshipped mountains, celestial bodies, ancestors, and the magnificent rock gorges and outcrops that make the scenery around Bogotá so exciting. The Muisca did not produce gold: they traded it from other tribes, and their gold objects tended to be small as a result. They could not have afforded the prodigal waste of gold dust described in the El Dorado legends. Thus, although there was religious significance in the mysterious Lake Guatavita, it was not central to Muisca beliefs. It is difficult to see how it could have given rise to the powerful El Dorado legend.

Others were not so skeptical. They believed along with Alexander von Humboldt that if sacrifices had been deposited in the lake over a period of many years, that untold treasures lay hidden in the lake bottoms. With almost as much persistence as the conquistadores of the sixteenth century, those who hunted for gold in the nineteenth century pursued their goal.

New Expeditions

In 1899, a London company called Contractors Limited began another assault on Lake Guatavita. One Englishman, W. Cooper, worked with a dozen Indian laborers for eight years on this project. Eventually they drained the lake. When Guatavita was nothing but a mass of mud, rivulets, and pools of water, they scoured the mud

"I am completely certain that the fabulous treasure of the Chibchas [is] to be found at the bottom of the lake [Guatavita]."

Gustavo Jaramillo Sánchez, twentieth-century miner and explorer

"The wealth supposedly beneath [Guatavita's] waters was never found."

Caspar Montibelli, *The World's Last Mysteries*

of the lake floor, prodding with sticks and occasionally finding Muisca objects. But the next day the sun had baked the mud to the consistency of concrete, so hard that it could not be penetrated. By the time the company obtained drilling equipment the lagoon had filled up again to its former level!

No one knows just how many expeditions have tried to conquer Guatavita and the other lakes in the northwestern wilds of South America, with little success. It seems almost as if some strange force is protecting whatever treasures may be concealed there. In his book *Gold & Silver, Silver & Gold*, Alvin Schwartz says, "People once believed that some buried treasures were haunted." Could this be the case with Lake Guatavita and the other sacred lakes?

Twentieth-Century Attempts

Even twentieth-century attempts to recover the treasure of the Chibchas have been thwarted.

In the 1950s, engineer and treasure hunter Kip Wagner decided Lake Guatavita was too cold to search for gold. In this picture, he is shown cleaning golden pieces of eight he found in a seventeenth-century Spanish shipwreck off the coast of Florida.

In 1949, Gustavo Jaramillo Sanchez tried to drag the lake with a clamshell-like device. In 1953, an American diver named Timperly scoured the lake with a steel ball with moveable claws. Another American, an experienced diver named Kip Wagner, entered the icy waters of Lake Guatavita and declared it was too cold for exploration.

"In all," writes author Caspar Montibelli, "the gold recovered by these expeditions was hardly sufficient to repay a fraction of the cost of the expeditions themselves."

Treasure that may still lie at the bottom of Lake Guatavita—or in other lakes in the vast wilderness called El Dorado—may be forever beyond reach.

But what of El Dorado, the city or kingdom of gold? Did it ever exist? Does it exist to this day? If so, why hasn't it been found?

El Dorado as a Place

More than once, conquistadors who braved steaming jungles, suffered intense cold in the mountains, and fought off the poison arrows of hostile Indians stopped just short of their goal. Why?

Antonio de Berrio was only four days' march from what he believed to be El Dorado at one point. Yet he moved on because he questioned the motives of the chief who had told him where the city was. Sir Walter Raleigh did not continue upstream past the falls of the Caroni River even though chief Topiawari said that was the way to El Dorado. Why did explorers turn back when they may have been so close to their goal? Perhaps the treasure hunters suspected that the Indians were sending them on wild goose chases. Perhaps it was easier to return to civilization and report that they had been very close to El Dorado than to return and say they had failed to discover where it was.

Treasures such as this beautiful golden ornament keep explorers on the trail of El Dorado.

Solid evidence of El Dorado as a realm of riches is hard to find. Indians from all the regions of northern South America insisted that a super city did exist. And certainly the conquistadores found temples sheathed in gold, life-sized golden idols, and palaces where royalty drank from gold cups and ate from golden plates. But was this enough? No! None of the cities in Peru, Colombia, or any other area seemed rich enough to qualify as the fabulous El Dorado.

Could it be that all the Spanish conquistadores, the English explorers, and the French and Dutch who followed them were merely looking in the wrong places? Maybe this golden city was further to the south and east than the conquistadores thought.

A Lost City in Brazil

On some maps of South America an area in the wilds of Brazil is included as part of "El Dorado." This area is known as the Matto Grosso. It is just to the east of Bolivia, in the very heart of the continent.

In his book *Among the Missing*, author Jay

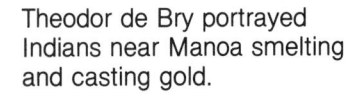

Theodor de Bry portrayed Indians near Manoa smelting and casting gold.

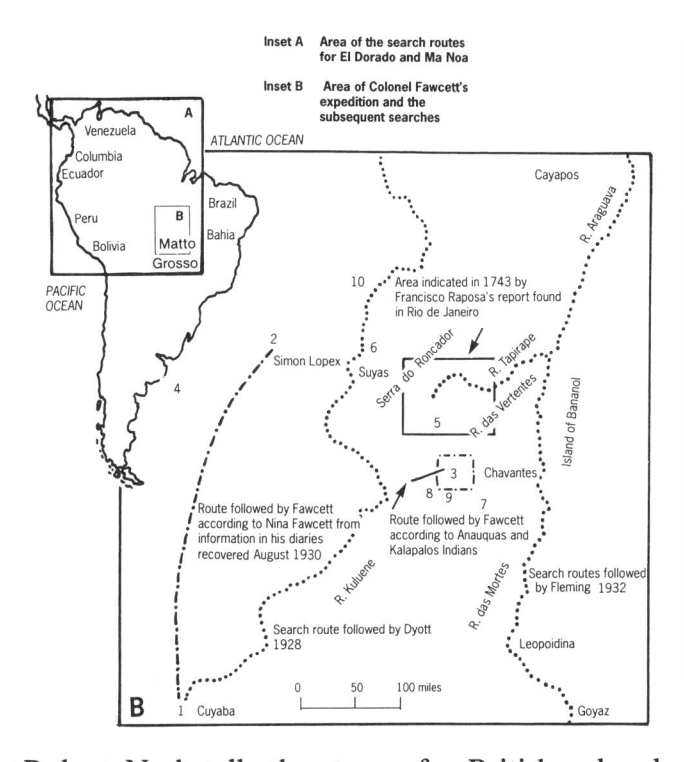

Inset A Area of the search routes for El Dorado and Ma Noa
Inset B Area of Colonel Fawcett's expedition and the subsequent searches

1. Colonel Fawcett's point of departure, 1925.
2. Fawcett's last message came from here.
3. Commander George Dyott's search for Fawcett came upon evidence. An Indian wearing a metal plate from Fawcett's trunk, 1928.
4. Fawcett reportedly was sighted here, dressed as an Indian, 1932.
5. Indians reported seeing Fawcett here; they had his compass, 1932.
6. A missionary said he had proof Fawcett died here, 1932.
7. Fawcett reportedly living here with son, 1933.
8. Indian chief confesses to having murdered Fawcett, 1946.
9. Skeleton found, declared to be Fawcett's, 1951.
10. 1952: A psychic medium claims to have contact with Fawcett who says he died peacefully here in 1935.

Robert Nash tells the story of a British colonel, Percy Harrison Fawcett, who entered this area in 1924 in search of a lost city that he believed lay hidden in this dark region. He based his belief on a document unearthed in the French national library about 1910. It told of a Portuguese expedition into the Matto Grosso in 1743. By accident, the Portuguese stumbled into a steep crevice and then climbed through an opening in a cliff wall. They followed ancient paved steps to a giant city in ruins. According to this document there was immense treasure, "both archaeological finds and precious stones." A nearby river actually glittered with massive gold deposits!

Only three of the men who left on that expedition returned. But the thought of danger did not deter Colonel Fawcett. Instead the story stirred him to probe the Brazilian jungle to find this lost city.

In the 1920s, Englishman Percy Harrison Fawcett set out to find El Dorado but never returned. This map shows part of his route as well as places he was rumored to have been seen.

> "Even today, in parts of Venezuela and Colombia, the belief still exists that somewhere, in the vast and unexplored region between the Orinoco and the Amazon, one may yet find the ruins of the famed city of El Dorado, and that there is still waiting there under the debris of crumbled palaces treasures as great as any ever found."
>
> H. J. Mozans, *The Quest of El Dorado*

> "The allure of El Dorado, the Golden Man, and Eldorado, the golden land, have lost their power over the minds of men.... They have been replaced by the reality of modern discoveries."
>
> Caspar Montibelli, *The World's Last Mysteries*

Fawcett's first attempt, in 1920, failed when his companions broke down. He all but had to drag them back to civilization. In 1924, he made a new plan. It included his son Jack and another young Englishman, Raleigh Rimmel. The three men traveled light as was Fawcett's habit. Author Jay Nash says, "Fawcett was no wild-eyed gold hunter motivated by greed, but a cautious, deliberate explorer whose aim was cultural discovery." Yet he was drawn "by a siren song he could not resist" into a place that for the most part is still uncharted today.

And he never returned. Nor did his companions.

Nash says, "Fawcett or his remains are as lost today...as the fabulous lost city he sought."

Was Fawcett's goal the same hidden city that became part of the El Dorado legend?

Will anyone ever find such a city or the wealth known as El Dorado?

If one went looking today, what would the chances be of finding gold?

Is There Treasure in El Dorado?

According to Tricia Haynes in *Let's Visit Colombia*, this country produces a large amount of gold and accounts for ninety-five percent of the world production of emeralds. Prospectors still search the river beds for treasure. But finding it is one thing—getting it out is another. Author Samuel Eliot Morison, in his book *The Great Explorers*, tells one reason visitors to the lands along the Equator have not always returned with full pockets:

> In 1940, when we were ranging this coast to check up on Columbus, we encountered an old prospector who explained why [this region] had never been really exploited for gold. Years before, he went up one of the rivers with a partner and an

Indian guide. 'Where do we find gold?' he asked, after paddling many miles. 'Right here!' said the Indian, who pulled out a clasp knife, dug some clay from the riverbank and panned out plenty of gold grains! The prospector and his partner began at once to plan how to spend their first million dollars. They returned to the nearest town for supplies and lumber and built sluice boxes (to channel water and catch gold), the product of which should have made them rich. But in the next freshet (a great rise in a stream caused by heavy rains) all this gear was washed into the Caribbean. That has happened again and again during the last four and a half centuries. There is still 'gold in them thar hills,' but only the Indians know how to get it out.

Six

The Lure of El Dorado

Author Jennifer Westwood writes in *The Atlas of Mysterious Places*, "As the Golden Man faded from memory, people assumed that his name applied to the place where unimaginable riches awaited them—Eldorado, hidden in the Andes or the Amazon jungle." Those who pursued the man or the place may have been right that it existed—or they may have been chasing a dream. Given the hazards to be encountered in the interior of South America, it is amazing that so many over so many decades continued the quest. Why did they persist?

In his book *Among the Missing*, Jay Robert Nash comments,

> Deep within most of us lurks the lust for riches. We seek the fabulous treasure troves, or sly business fortunes, or inheritances rendered in the dark. Countless hordes have stalked El Dorado and thousands of other fantasy pits of wealth that subtly encourage the patience and persistence of the seeker on the promise of yielding that inevitable pot of gold. The anticipation of discovery is the magic lure, the fine madness in which many have become lost inside their golden pursuits. It is not always a matter of hidden treasure; the motives of these [who pursue so relentlessly] are often vague, sometimes totally inexplicable.

To Nash's way of thinking, then, it is the *promise*

An old map shows a possible location of El Dorado at Manoa.

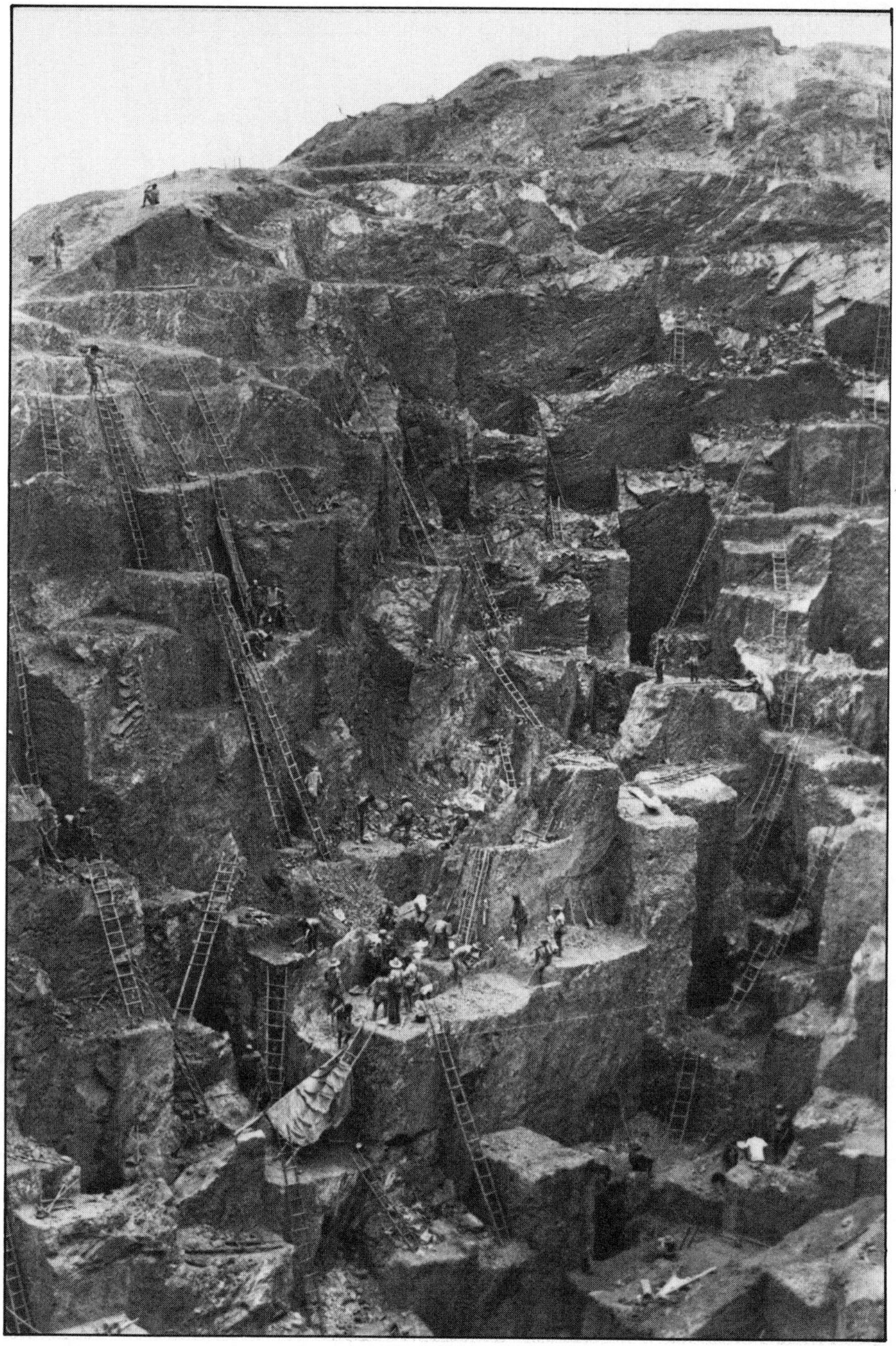

that keeps treasure hunters on the trail.

As a promise, El Dorado is often a synonym for paradise, or utopia—any place where dreams may come true. El Dorado may be only a destination of the mind, an unattainable goal. But there is a certain magic in the word itself. Perhaps residents of El Dorado County, California, or Eldorado Street in Decatur, Illinois, were lured to their homes by a dream that they would find happiness there. Maybe people who buy a Cadillac Eldorado expect to get a luxury car that will bring them delight.

The story of the cacique covered in gold dust is no doubt the inspiration for the following phrases in Stephen Birnbaum's tourist guide, *South America 1989*:

> Float on a lake in a boat made of reeds...hang in a hammock near the Amazon's source...dive for gold in a bottomless lake...

One does not need to know the legend to be enticed. However, enough people do connect El Dorado to gold and glory that the term is often used to attract interest. Author Jonathan Kandell called his recent book about the wilderness areas of South America *Passage Through El Dorado*. The title is tantalizing, but the Golden Man is used merely to stir the reader's imagination. Kandell does not claim to guide his readers to that fabulous lost city.

Does this mean that El Dorado the Golden Man and El Dorado the golden land are just words now? Have they lost their original power to pull people into hazardous situations from which they may never return?

No!

Archaeologist Konrad Krans, of Coon Rapids, Minnesota, says, "South America is full of people looking for Eldorado." His own last trip was in 1970. He and a friend, Stan Sroga,

---

"A hundred separate stories and legends became confused into one hypnotic legend."

Caspar Montibelli, *The World's Last Mysteries*

"We have no reason to plume ourselves on our superior knowledge....Had we lived in their day we should have belonged either to the many wise men who believed as they did, or to the many foolish men who not only sneered at the story of El Dorado but at a hundred other stories which we now know to be true."

H. J. Mozans, *The Quest of El Dorado*

Opposite: In the early 1980s, a huge gold strike occurred at Serra Pelada, Brazil. Gold is still being mined there. Might this have been the source of the fabled gold of El Dorado?

Konrad Krans, a Minnesota archaeologist, is one of many twentieth-century explorers who have fruitlessly sought El Dorado.

went to Colombia and Ecuador, admittedly looking for whatever treasure they could find.

The Search Today

Krans had read about the capture of Atahualpa by Francisco Pizarro in 1532, and he had also ferreted out information that much of the ransom intended for the cacique's release never reached Cuzco. When loyal subjects of the Inca chief heard that Pizarro had killed their king, they dumped the ransom along the roads in the Andes Mountains. Krans says, "Huge amounts of gold were left along the roads. This is fact, not fantasy." Of course, most of it is gone by now, but some may remain, hidden in underbrush or covered by earth. It is a powerful lure.

Krans and his colleague financed their trip themselves. They explored with the help of natives, who, Sroga says, "were only too eager to offer their services to any tourists who looked as if they might be searching for adventure."

The natives led Krans and Sroga to grave sites where, with large pointed rods, they probed for treasures that were traditionally buried with the dead. It was not easy. Much digging was involved, and, like the conquistadores of old, they were plagued by the climate. "It rains all the time," says Krans. "It's a terrible place. It's swampy, muddy, there are flash floods. You have nothing to eat but what you bring in yourself. And there are nasty bears! They're called spectacled bears, and they're like grizzlies. This is the only place in the world where they're found. We never saw them but we heard them groaning at night and saw their huge droppings in the morning."

When Krans recalls his adventures it is the work and discomfort he remembers. "We were constantly whacking our way through dense vegetation," he says, "because this is cloud

A drawing of an Incan burial. Food, household objects, and golden items were buried with the dead.

forest. We felt ghastly all the time!"

From the village of Pillaro, south of Quito, Krans brought back "a couple tons of artifacts." Most were in the form of pottery. He found only a little gold, and what he found was not solid, but mixed with copper. Yet he calls this a successful trip.

Junius Bird, a famous archaeologist, flew out to Minnesota to inspect the find and chose many of the pieces of pottery for the Museum of Natural History in New York City. The rest was sold to a lawyer in Washington, D.C., who planned to give it to a university.

Krans continues to collect artifacts, but now confines his trips to Mexico and Central America. Asked about the treasures to be found today in El Dorado, he replies, "Atahualpa's gold is still there."

The Search Goes On

Will someone, someday find the gold? Will someone, someday find El Dorado?

Perhaps. Perhaps not. But chances are good the desire for El Dorado will never die.

A piece of the treasure of El Dorado.

> Through sunshine and shadow,
> From darkness to noon,
> Over mountains that reach
> From the sky to the moon,
> A man with a dream that
> He'll never let go,
> Keeps searching to find El Dorado.
>
> > -Words of the theme song from the movie *El Dorado* produced by Paramount Pictures

Bibliography

Stephen Birnbaum, Editor, *Birnbaum's South America 1989*. Boston: Houghton Mifflin, 1988.

Warwick Bray, *The Gold of El Dorado*. London: Times Newspapers Limited, 1978.

Christopher Caldwell, Audrey Liounis, and Alice Thompson, Editors, *Fodor's South America 1988*. New York: Fodor's Travel Publications, Inc., 1987.

Thomas Dickey, John Man, and Henry Wiencek, *The Kings of El Dorado*. Chicago: Stonehenge Press, 1982.

Ferol Egan, *The El Dorado Trail*. New York: McGraw-Hill, 1970.

Charles F. Gritzner, *Guyana in Pictures*. Minneapolis: Lerner Publications Company, 1988.

Tricia Haynes, *Let's Visit Colombia*. London: Burke Publishing Company, 1985.

John Hemming, *The Search for El Dorado*. New York: E. P. Dutton, 1978.

Jonathan Kandell, *Passage Through El Dorado: Traveling the World's Last Great Wilderness*. New York: William Morrow and Company, 1984.

Caspar Montibelli, *The World's Last Mysteries*. New York: Reader's Digest Association, 1978.

Samuel Eliot Morison, *The Great Explorers: The European Discovery of America*. New York: Oxford University Press, 1978.

H. J. Mozans, *The Quest of El Dorado*. New York: D. Appleton and Company, 1917.

V. S. Naipaul, *The Loss of El Dorado*. London: André Deutsch, 1969.

Jay Robert Nash, *Among the Missing*. New York: Simon and Schuster, 1978.

Harriet Rohmer and Jesús Guerrero Rea (adapted by), *The Treasure of Guatavita*. San Francisco: Children's Book Press, 1978.

Alvin Schwartz. *Gold & Silver, Silver & Gold*. New York: Farrar Straus Giroux, 1988.

Timothy Severin, *The Golden Antilles*. New York: Alfred A. Knopf, 1970.

Victor W. von Hagen, *The Golden Man: A Quest for El Dorado*. Hampshire, England: D. C. Heath, 1974.

Jennifer Westwood, Editor, *The Atlas of Mysterious Places*, New York: Weidenfeld & Nicolson, 1987.

Index

Albujar, Juan Martinez de
  story of gilded man, 70-72, 74
Amazon River, 61-62, 66
Amazon women, 63-66
Atahualpa
  Inca Chief, 36, 37, 40, 50, 51, 104
Atlantic Ocean
  search for waterway across, 18, 19
Aztec Indians
  golden gifts to Cortez, 26-28

Balboa, Vasco Núñez de
  discovery of Pacific Ocean, 25-26
  search for gold, 23-25
Bastidás, Rodrigo de, 22-23
Belalcázar, Sebastian de
  search for gilded man, 50-53, 54, 56
Berrio, Antonio de
  and Sir Walter Raleigh, 74-76, 79
  search for gilded man, 68-70, 72-73, 95
Bogotá, Colombia, 40, 48, 53, 56
Bolivia
  search for gold in, 37-39
Brazil
  search for gold in, 96-98

cacique
  definition of, 10
cannibals
  in the New World, 24, 25
Carvajal, Gaspar de, 62-65, 66
Castillo, Bernal Diaz del, 27
Cathay, *see* China
Central America
  first permanent Spanish settlement, 23-24
Charles V, King of Spain, 28, 68
Chibcha Indians, 33, 42, 68
  religious practices of, 10, 12, 48, 53-54, 92-93
China as land of riches, 16, 18
Christian missionaries
  and conversion of natives, 26
Cieza, Pedro de, 53
cinnamon, search for, 47, 58-59
Cipangu, *see* Japan
Colombia
  as a source of gold, 40, 48, 56, 98
  see also Lake Guatavita
Columbus, Christopher, 13
  search for gold, 19-22
  search for passage to Indies, 16, 18
conquistadores, definition of, 23
Contractors Limited
  search of Lake Guatavita, 93-94
Cortéz, Hernando
  search for gold in Mexico, 26-28
Cosa, Juan de la, 22-23
Cuzco, Peru, 36-37

Dabeiba, Chief, 24-25, 26
Dalfinger, Ambrosius
  search for gold, 29-34, 35
Darien, Panama, 23-24

El Dorado
  and the religious ritual of, 10, 12, 48-49
  explanation of, 15, 101, 103
  myths about, 13, 15, 23, 26, 40, 42-43, 44-45, 46-49, 100
  searches for, 50-56, 58-61, 67-77, 86-93, 96-99
Ewaipanoma Indians, myths about, 81

Fawcett, Percy Harrison
  search for gold, 97-98
Federmann, Nicolaus
  search for gilded man, 54-56
Ferdinand and Isabella, King and Queen of Spain
  authorize settlement of Sinú region, 23
  finance Columbus, 18, 19, 21
Ferdinand II, King of Spain
  and Balboa, 25
Freyle, Juan Rodríguez, 44, 49, 89

gold, mystique of, 16
Golden City, myths about, 46-49
Golden Man
  myths about, 10-15, 16, 34, 40, 42-43, 44-45, 52, 54, 71-72
  see also El Dorado
Gómara, Francisco López de, 66
Guiana, 74, 77, 81, 84

Haiti, discovery of, 21, 22
Hemming, John, 23
  description of South American jungle, 56
  description of Amazon river, 62
  on Amazon tribes, 44
  on Amazon women, 66
  on Sebastian de Belalcázar, 52,

on Ambrosius Dalfinger, 32-35
on origin of El Dorado, 40, 46-47
on Guiana, 67-68
on Muisca tunjo, 92-93
on Sir Walter Raleigh, 85
on search of Lake Guatavita, 42, 88, 89
Hispaniola, *see* Haiti

Inca Empire, 35, 40, 50-51, 59, 76
India as land of riches, 16

Japan as land of riches, 16, 19, 21
Jirajara Indians, 30

Kandell, Jonathan, 39, 103
Keymis, Captain, 79, 85
Krans, Konrad
search for gold, 103-105

Lake Guatavita (n. Colombia)
and Chibcha religious myth, 10, 12, 16, 42, 44, 49, 54
gold found in, 88
searches for gold in, 48, 88-90, 93-95
Lake Maracaibo, 31, 33, 35
Lake Siecha
search for gold in, 92

Martin, Esteban, 30, 31, 32
Martin, Francisco, 34-35
Matto Grosso, Brazil, 96, 97
Mexico
search for gold in, 26-28
Montezuma, 26
Montibelli, Caspar, 53, 54, 55, 86, 95
Morison, Samuel Eliot, 22, 98
Muiscas Indians, *see* Chibcha Indians

Naipaul, V. S., 70, 71, 72
Nash, Jay Robert, 96-98, 100

Ocean Sea, *see* Atlantic Ocean
Orellana, Francisco de
search for gilded man, 60-64, 66-67
Orinoco Indians, 47, 48, 68
Orinoco River
as a road to El Dorado, 68-69, 72-75, 77-79, 85
Oviedo, Basillo Vicente de, 48, 49
Oviedo, Fernández de, 42-43, 49

Pacabueyes Indians, 31-32, 34
Pacific Ocean
discovery of, 25-26
Parima Lake, 84
Pay-titi, 37, 39
Perez, Demetrio Ramos, 42

Peru
and search for gold, 35-37
Philip II, 73
Pizarro, Francisco
search for gold, 35-37, 40, 47, 50, 58, 104
Pizarro, Gonzalo
search for gold and cinnamon, 47, 58-60
Polo, Marco, 18-19
Popayan, 52
Putijma, Chief, 79

Quesada, Gonzalo Jiménez de
search for gilded man, 48, 53-56, 68
Quito, Ecuador, 42, 46-49, 52, 58-59

Raleigh, Sir Walter
book about search, 81-83
search for gilded man, 73-80, 95
second voyage, 84-85

salt, search for, 48
Sanchez, Gustavo Jaramillo, 95
Schwartz, Alvin, 68-69, 94
Sepúlveda, Antonio
search of Lake Guatavita, 86, 88-89, 90
Severin, Timothy, 12
on Juan Martinez de Albujar, 71
on Antonio de Berrio, 68
on ceremony at Lake Guatavita, 12, 42
on legend of El Dorado, 40
on Sir Walter Raleigh, 74, 78, 82, 85
Simon, Pedro, 88
Sinú region, 23
South America
early description of, 56-57
religious ritual of the Golden Man, 10, 12
search for gold in, 29-39, 50-56
Spain
and conquistadores' search for gold, 16-39
Sroga, Stan, 103-104

Teuhtlilli, 26, 27
Topiawari, Chief, 76-77, 79, 95
Trinidad, 75, 78
tunjos, 88, 92

Vascuña, Iñigo de, 34, 35
Vera, Domingo de, 72-73
von Hagen, Victor, 13, 28, 52, 54, 55, 60, 66, 84
on Amazon women, 66
on Sebastian de Belalcázar, 52, 54
on Ambrosius Dalfinger, 29-31
on Nicolaus Federmann, 55
on gold in New World, 28
on Golden Man, 13
on Gonzalo Pizarro, 60

on search of Lake Guatavita, 88, 90
on Sir Walter Raleigh, 84
von Humboldt, Alexander
 and search of Lake Guatavita, 89-90, 93

Wagner, Kip, 95
Welser company
 trade with the Indies, 28, 54
Westwood, Jennifer, 16, 100
Wiencek, Henry, 92

Picture Credits

Courtesy Museo del Oro (Bogotá), 11, 27b, 41, 57, 92, 196
From *Americae achter theil* by Theodor de Bry (1599), 12, 17, 25t, 33t, 63, 75, 77, 96
Mary Ahrndt, 14, 23, 49, 55b, 71, 84, 89, 97
The Mansell Collection, 18, 29t, 55t, 67, 73, 74
The Granger Collection, 20, 25b, 34, 44, 56, 101
The Bettmann Archive, 22, 26, 27t, 36t, 91, 102
From *El descubrimiento del oceano pacifico...* by Jose Toribio Medina (Santiago, Chile: 1913), 24
Courtesy the British Library: from *Codex Köler*, Add. 15217 folio 37, 29b. From *Codex Köler* Add. 15217 folio 40v, 30. From *Travels* by Levinus Hulsius (1599), 64, 66, 68, 82
From *Nueva coronica y buen gobierno* by Felipe Guaman Poma de Ayala, 37
From *La Edad del oro*, Edicion de Jose Miguel Oviedo (Barcelona: Tusquets Editores, 1986), 38
From *De Aanmerkenswaardigste zee-en landreizen* by Pieter van de Aa (1727), 42
From *Vue des Cordillères et monument des peuples indigènes de l'Amerique* by Alexander von Humboldt (Paris: 1810), 45, 51
From *The mysterious world: an atlas of the unexplained* by Francis Hitching (New York: Holt Rinehart and Winston, 1978), 46
Anna Zuckerman/PhotoEdit, 48
From *Sebastian de Belalcazar, fundador de ciudades 1490-1551*, by Diego Garces Giraldo (Cali, Colombia: D. Garces Giraldo, 1986), 52
Ardea London Ltd., 54, 69
Courtesy Minneapolis Public Library, Picture Collection, 58
From *The golden dream; seekers of El Dorado* by Walker Chapman (New York: Bobbs-Merrill, 1967), 61, 80
Courtesy The Royal Geographical Society, 62
From *The quest of El Dorado...* by John Augustine Zahm (New York: Appleton, 1917), 70, 76, 87
From *Historia general de las Indias* by Hernandez de Oviedo (Seville: 1535), 78
From *The discoverie of the large, rich and bewtiful empyre of Guiana* by Sir Walter Raleigh (London: 1596), 81
From *Travels* by Levinus Hulsius (1599), 83
AP/Wide World Photos, 94, 95
Courtesy Konrad Krans, 104

About the Author

Norma Gaffron, a former school teacher, lives in New Brighton, Minnesota.

Norma has been writing professionally for the past dozen years. Her articles, on topics as diverse as sailing, snakes, and replanting lost teeth, have appeared in many national magazines. She has been a Junior Great Books leader and is regional advisor for the National Society of Children's Book Writers. She and her husband have three grown children.

Norma likes to write and to explore ideas that hover on the fringe of reality. She says, "I am fascinated by the sheer persistence of the conquistadores who pursued El Dorado, and by the fact that there are golden treasures still hidden in secret places somewhere in the land called El Dorado."

El Dorado: Land of Gold is Norma's fourth book in the Great Mysteries series.